W9-DCE-950

Livonia Public Library
ALFRED NOBLE BRANCH
32901 PLYMOUTH ROAD
Livonia, Michigan 48150

973.022
D

Slosson, Preston William, 1892-
    Pictorial history of the American people /
Preston W. Slosson. -- Rev. ed. -- New York :
Gallery Books, c1985.
    328 p. : ill.
    ISBN 0-8317-6871-1 : 15.98

    1. United States--History--Pictorial works.
2. United States--Description and travel--
Views.

                        39290

                                         Ja86

19

PICTORIAL
HISTORY OF THE
AMERICAN
PEOPLE

Catholics and Calvinists in Bohemia but ended as an attempt to extend the frontiers of France, a Catholic country, but allied to Protestant Sweden because of a common fear of Catholic Austria and Spain.

Politically, Europe was entering the period of national monarchy. Most states in the Middle Ages had been monarchies in form, but royal authority was weakened by the power of the warrior nobility, the Catholic clergy and the autonomy of certain city-states which, especially in Germany, the Netherlands and Italy, were almost independent. The so-called Holy Roman Empire, mainly but not exclusively German, had failed to achieve European unity.

Real power settled more and more in the rulers of countries which, in the main, had a common speech and a common national tradition. England, Scotland, France, Spain, Portugal, Denmark, Sweden, Russia and Turkey (the only non-Christian power in Europe) tended to conform to this pattern. The invention of the cannon weakened the power of the armored cavalry and the stone castles of the nobility; the controversies of the Reformation weakened the political influence of the clergy. As for the commercial middle classes in the towns, they often preferred the single law of a monarch to the confusion of feudal nobles, and sided with the king.

There were some exceptions to this general rule. The Swiss repelled the Austrians and Burgundians from their Alpine strongholds and emerged as an independent republic. With greater difficulty, the Netherlands shook off the combined religious and political tyranny of Spain. Poland remained in its feudal condition as an aristocracy of nobles with an elective kingship. England, though strongly centralized under the Tudor dynasty from Henry VII to Elizabeth I, preserved its elected Parliament, and in the 17th century briefly established a republic (the Commonwealth) under the dictatorship of Oliver Cromwell. Later, with the return of the Stuart dynasty, there was a compromise in the tacit condition that, while the king might reign, it was the landed aristocracy, represented by Parliament, which really ruled.

One more fact remains to be mentioned which had a great bearing on the settlement of America. This was the coming of capitalism and commercialism. In the Middle Ages, tenants paid their master chiefly in labor or a share of the crops (like the modern 'sharecropper' in the South) and very little in actual cash. But as money became more abundant and circulated more rapidly, it was more convenient for both landlord and tenant to substitute simple rent for feudal services.

THE GREAT EXPLORATIONS

Almost certainly the first Europeans to visit America were Norwegian and Icelandic Vikings who sailed westward about AD 1000. They reported a 'Markland,' or land of woods, and a 'Vinland,' or land of grapes. How far south they ventured we do not know, but vestiges of their temporary settlements have been recently found in Newfoundland. They were among the most venturesome of men, sailing in open boats with but a single sail to lands completely unknown. In Europe they showed the same boldness, raiding Scotland, Ireland and England; settling in northern France (Normandy) and Sicily and enlisting in the Varangian bodyguard of the Greek emperors of Constantinople. They also gave a name to Russia.

But their western discoveries were not followed up by settlements, except in coastal Greenland which eventually passed to the hands of Denmark. They seem to have been unknown in most of Europe at the time, and scholars doubt that Columbus was aware of them. American history really begins with the voyage of this Genoese explorer, Christopher Columbus, in the service of Spain.

Geographers had long known that the earth was spherical, and thus one could reach the Far East by sailing to the west. Already, under the command of the Portuguese Henry the Navigator, ships had cautiously sailed down the African west coast, seeking an all-water route around southern Africa. They had resources which the Vikings lacked: the compass, maps of the eastern Atlantic and Mediterranean shores, and covered decks.

But most men were not scholars. Sailors for such a voyage were hard to recruit. How to return to Europe if one sailed downhill to the other side of the world? Suppose one were to drop off into space? What if one encountered impossible dangers? One medieval writer had declared the sun was red in the evening because 'she looketh down into Hell.' Better play it safe and hug familiar shores.

Queen Isabella of Castile, whose marriage to Ferdinand of Aragon had united Spain, secured loans which financed the expedition. Almost at the same time, the Spaniards conquered Granada, the last Moorish stronghold. The great day of Spanish power had arrived.

Opposite left: Sixteenth century sailors were able to chart their course by observing the stars.
Opposite right: Those great navigators, the Norsemen, would often beach their boats and use them as shelter. *Above:* On his first voyage of exploration, Christopher Columbus landed at San Salvador (now known as Watling Island) in the central area of the Bahamas on 12 October 1492. The expedition had been financed in 1492 by King Ferdinand and Queen Isabella of Spain, who earlier that year had finally managed to conquer the final Moorish outpost in their country at Granada and had expelled Jews who refused to accept Catholicism.

Columbus first reached some of the West Indies islands in 1492. In subsequent voyages he extended the knowledge of the Caribbean area, but he never reached any part of the present United States. An Englishman of Venetian descent, John Cabot, discovered Newfoundland (the new found land) and thus laid the cornerstone for the British overseas empire. But the early discoveries were largely Spanish and Portuguese. Ferdinand Magellan was the first to attempt a voyage around the whole world; he died in passage, but one of his ships completed the circuit. Pope Alexander VI divided the colonial world between Spain and Portugal, giving America to Spain and Africa, India and eastern Brazil to Portugal. Naturally, the Protestant nations such as England and Holland paid him no attention, and even Catholic France colonized within American territory.

England undertook no settlement until James I, but the Elizabethan period may be said to have 'cleared the way' for an empire by winning the mastery of the sea and defeating the Spanish Armada in 1588. It is a curious thing to note that many national claims were based upon explorations made by foreigners. Columbus and Cabot were of Italian origin. Magellan, Portuguese by birth, enabled Spain to gain the Philippines (the Islands of King Philip). Henry Hudson, an Englishman, by his discoveries in the river valley which bears his name, made possible the Dutch colony of New Netherland (now New York).

In their thirst for gold, the Spaniards built a great American empire. Hernando Cortez in Mexico and Francisco Pizarro in Peru were the chief *conquistadores* (conquerers). Hernando de Soto added Florida.

It is another interesting fact that the colonizing nations sought homes as much like their native European ones as possible. Thus Spain, a rugged mountainous peninsula, struck boldly overland; France, a land of great rivers, followed the Mississippi, Ohio and St Lawrence valleys; the Dutch, Portuguese and English, who live near the sea, at first kept to the shorelines or the islands.

All the exploring nations sought gold and silver, but only the Spaniards found much of either. Their treasure ships brought back stores of bullion to Spain, which eventually passed into general circulation in Europe, increasing prices and wages and hastening the coming of free contracts on a cash basis, and the business of banking.

Failing to find gold and silver, the colonizing nations sought other commodities which could be traded for them. The English, for example, found sugar cane and tobacco useful staples in the South and furs, fish and forest timber in the North. The Dutch brought back from the East Indies wealth in spices and even tentatively began to trade with China and Japan. In the early 19th century, cotton from the South became the chief American export, but this was of less importance in the colonial period.

The new continent should have been called *Columbia* (or perhaps *Ericsonia*, after the Norse explorer, Leif Ericson). Actually it bears the name of a Florentine geographer and navigator, Amerigo Vespucci. He was an able mapmaker, one of the first to realize that the New World was not an eastern wing of the Old, but a continent in its own right, and his name became attached to it. It hardly matters, for the name of Columbus is given to a South American nation, to our federal capital district, and to many a city in the United States.

Left: Henry Hudson, the English explorer, sailed up the river valley that bears his name. The Dutch explorers took advantage of his discoveries and founded the settlement of New Netherland, which became New York when the British gained control of the area. *Top:* Vasco Nuñez de Balboa, the Spanish explorer, discovered the Pacific Ocean and claimed dominion over the South Seas for Spain. *Above:* Hernando Cortez, the conqueror of Mexico, was first received by the Aztec emperor, Montezuma, in a style befitting a foreign dignitary. *Opposite page, above:* Hernando de Soto of Spain discovered the Mississippi River and claimed what is now the state of Florida for the Spanish crown. *Right:* An early Spanish settlement in Florida.

VIRGINIA AND THE SOUTH

Virginia (1607) is the oldest of the 13 colonies – Georgia (1733) the youngest. All the southern colonies bear in their names the time of their origin. Virginia celebrates the 'Virgin Queen,' Elizabeth I; Maryland, Queen Mary II; the two Carolinas, King Charles II; Georgia, King George.

They had a warm climate suitable for staple plantation crops which could be worked by slave labor. All the colonies recognized slavery, but in the more northern colonies, a region of cold winters, small farms and commercial occupations, slavery was less profitable and eventually died out. Some northern colonies, however, shared with England and the South the shipment of black slaves from Africa.

No permanent settlement was made in Elizabeth's time, though there was much exploration and some abortive attempts at colonization. The first settlement was made at Jamestown in the reign of James I under the auspices of the Virginia Company of London. It was kept alive, under great difficulties, by the vigorous activity of Capt John Smith. He had a romantic disposition, and may have been something of a romancer in his narratives. All Americans know the story of his rescue by Pocahontas, an Indian maiden, who later married, not Smith, but one of his comrades, John Rolfe.

In 1619, the year when Virginia was settled, a legislative body was constituted, slavery was introduced, and a group of young women was brought over to become the wives of the settlers. There was no absolute compulsion to marry, but the women knew what to expect and the men eagerly awaited their coming. Often the dowry was paid in tobacco, the staple crop.

Eventually the company charter was revoked and direct royal authority established. A 'House of Burgesses' represented the voters of the colony. The capitol was established at Williamsburg, where many of the old buildings still stand and some others have been restored. Governor William Berkeley, who boasted that Virginia contained no printing presses or free schools, ruled so harshly that he provoked the rebellion

Left: John White, the cartographer on Sir Walter Raleigh's expedition to the New World in 1585, created a map of the area around the settlement of Roanoke, in what is now the state of Virginia. *Top:* Pocahontas, the daughter of Chief Powhatan, was taken to England where, at the age of 21 in 1616, she was painted while wearing an Elizabethan English costume. *Above:* An engraving of the legend of the rescue of Capt John Smith by Pocahontas. *Opposite top:* The Old Bruton Parish Church in Williamsburg, Virginia was completed in 1715. *Right:* One of the most popular sports of the outdoorsmen of Virginia and Maryland during the colonial period was riding to the hounds on a fox hunt.

19

of Nathaniel Bacon. Reprisals were taken against the rebels, and so many were hanged that Charles II impatiently said, 'That old fool has put more men to death in that naked country than I did in all England for the murder of my father.'

Virginia was mainly royalist and Anglican, but Bacon's rebellion showed that there were limits to its tolerance. The colony played a large part in the preliminaries of the American Revolution in Patrick Henry, and it furnished the sword of the Revolution in George Washington and the pen of the Revolution in Thomas Jefferson. Most of the settlers were English, but there were some Germans and Scotch-Irish.

All in all, Virginia may be said to have been not only the first in origin, but the first in influence during the colonial times and in the earliest years of the republic.

Maryland was the undertaking of Lord Baltimore, whose name is preserved in the name of its chief city. Like Virginia, its staple crop was tobacco. Lord Baltimore desired tolerance for his fellow Roman Catholics, but also established tolerance for all Christians. There was difficulty in determining the boundaries of the new colony, but eventually two surveyors, Charles Mason and Jeremiah Dixon, drew the line between Maryland and Pennsylvania. As Pennsylvania became a free state, this 'Mason-Dixon Line' became famous as the northern boundary of slavery.

North and South Carolina were curiously different. South Carolina – wealthy and aristocratic, a region of great slave plantations – in some respects resembled the colonies of the West Indies rather than those of the American mainland. North Carolina was more a region of small farms and relatively poor men, and it had no large cities such as Charleston in South Carolina.

Georgia was a philanthropic enterprise of James Oglethorpe, who wanted to find a home for distressed debtors and religious refugees. In his original plans there was to be no slavery, no intoxicating liquor, and a concentration on growing silk, grapes, medicinal plants and other commodities lacking in England. All these restrictions were later abandoned, and Georgia became a typical southern slave state.

Although slavery has long ceased to exist, the South remains, in many respects, unique as compared with the rest of the nation. It is still mainly agricultural. There has been, as everywhere, some urbanization, but far less than in the North. People still live an open-air life and are accustomed to ride, hunt and shoot.

Above left: The port of Baltimore in the Colony of Maryland was a thriving little community in 1752. *Above:* A painting of Cecil Calvert with his grandson. He was the second Lord Baltimore, following George Calvert, the Roman Catholic founder of Maryland. *Above center:* Another example of settlers coming to the colonies to escape religious intolerance were the Tyrolean Lutherans. They had been persecuted in Salzburg, in what is now Austria, a Roman Catholic city, and emigrated to Georgia. *Right:* The English philanthropist James Oglethorpe founded the Colony of Georgia in 1733 as a home for debtors and religious refugees. He is shown introducing a group of Georgia Indians in London in 1734 to the trustees of the colony.

In the early republic, the South, although scarcely having one-third of the population, took a great part in the nation's leadership, both in peace and war. Of the first 12 presidents, nine were from the South; and of the first five, Virginia supplied four. Though the Civil War reduced southern political leadership, it may be ventured that a fair half of the most distinguished army officers in all American wars had a southern background.

The colonial South was aristocratic in attitude. Although most of its 'first families' were of recent origin, few were of the English gentry, and almost none of the nobility, cared to emigrate to the colonies. They lived a more leisurely life and had a wider range of amusements than most settlers farther north. Some were religious Deists, accepting the creation but denying the authority of the Bible. It was a later development that caused H L Mencken to label the South as the 'Bible Belt.' The white population of the South, although it contained some Germans, French Huguenots and Scotch-Irish pioneers, was more purely English than elsewhere. Most European immigrants had gone to the cities of the North.

NEW ENGLAND AND THE PURITANS

In a sense, all the American colonies of England constituted a 'New England,' but custom restricts the term to the six states east of New York; Massachusetts, Connecticut, Rhode Island, Vermont, New Hampshire and Maine. Of these, only four existed in colonial times; Maine was later formed from Massachusetts territory and Vermont from land disputed between New Hampshire and New York.

To understand New England, one must begin with the Puritan movement in Old England. The Puritans were not a denomination, although on American soil most of them formed Congregational churches in which government was vested in the general body of members of each congregation. In England some were members of the established Anglican Church who wished to simplify ritual, diminish episcopal authority and promote the doctrines of Calvin. They wanted to 'purify' Protestantism of all that suggested Roman ritual. They adhered to a code of austere personal conduct, and most of them disapproved of 'worldly amusements' such as card playing, ballroom dancing and the theater. They were strongest in the towns and cities, especially in the eastern counties of England, and among the so-called middle classes.

In England they opposed the autocratic policies and church doctrines of King James I and Charles I. In 1642 they rebelled against Charles and established a short-lived republic, absorbing Scotland and Ireland and the American colonies. Cromwell assented to the execution of King Charles in 1649. He tried to establish a liberal and fairly democratic policy, but all his attempts were balked by the fact that the Puritans did not represent a real majority. Most Englishmen wanted the old traditional government by 'king, lords and commons,' and, though they had resented Charles's attempt to get along without Parliament, they also had no love for a Puritan military dictatorship. So, in 1660, Charles's son, Charles II, was reinstated on the throne.

In the reign of King James I, some Puritans exiled themselves to the Netherlands where they enjoyed the religious freedom denied them in England. But they felt that their children might lose their English heritage. Was there some place where they could find both Puritanism and an English atmosphere? Yes, in the American wilderness. So the Plymouth Chartered Company sailed in the *Mayflower* to the northern part of Virginia, as yet unsettled, in 1620. They are known as the 'Pilgrim Fathers.' A much larger and wealthier community of Puritans settled around Boston in 1630.

Since they sought religious truth as they saw it, rather than religious freedom for its own sake, they expelled various heretics and limited the

Top left: The Pilgrims, a group of English and Dutch Calvinists, wanted to emigrate to a place where they could have religious freedom. In this illustration by Currier and Ives, they are shown landing at Plymouth on 11 December 1620. The ship *Mayflower* is in the distance. *Top right:* The center of Massachusetts Bay Colony, Boston, had many grand churches that were built in the 18th century: Christ Church as illustrated in 1723. *Above:* Boston was a flourishing city in the 1750s. This view shows the main square. The Old State House on State Street in the center of the painting

still stands, as do many
of the other buildings.
Top: The Puritans were a
deeply religious group.
In this painting by
Boughton, they are going
through the woods to a
Sunday service.

vote to church members of good standing. Roger Williams, a Baptist, who favored the complete separation of church and state, settled in Providence, Rhode Island; Ann Hutchinson in Connecticut. The Quakers were not tolerated and many had to find a refuge in Pennsylvania.

The colonists in the Massachusetts colony had a magnificent concept – that education was important. They established universal education and required towns to maintain schools. They founded the first American university, Harvard, named for one of its early benefactors.

Of course, the Puritan theocracy could not stand indefinitely. The British government might suffer Congregationalists if they were as far away as America, but could hardly sanction discrimination against Anglicans. Moreover, some of the later arrivals had more interest in making a living than in questions of doctrine. One Puritan leader reminded the people of a fishing settlement that their fathers had come to New England for purity of faith. A dissident arose and said, 'You must be thinking of the people down at the Bay. *Our* chief aim was to catch fish.' The Puritan was turning into the Yankee.

A blot upon the Puritan record was an outbreak of witchcraft panic in Salem in which 19 persons were executed. But the New Englanders were more merciful than many Europeans, such as those in Germany and Scotland, in hanging the supposed witches instead of burning them. Moreover, Samuel Sewall, one of the judges, becoming convinced of his error, did an annual penance on the anniversary of his erring decision.

What is a 'Yankee'? Many Europeans apply the term to all people from the United States, much to the annoyance of the person from Mississippi or Alabama. In turn, it may mean anyone from the North. But, properly speaking, it means only the New Englander and will here be used in this sense.

The word calls up the image of a peddler carrying a pack of 'Yankee notions' for sale – an industrious, thrifty man, turning a penny many times until it becomes a shilling. Or, perhaps, it means a young 'schoolmaam' holding a blue-backed speller before a class of children. New England was the teacher of the nation's teachers.

Most New Englanders were farmers, but many were cod fishermen, shipbuilders and merchants. They were eminent in all the professions. This tiny and rather bleak corner of the country has probably produced as many outstanding poets, essayists, historians, philosophers and natural scientists as has all the rest of the United States. If it yielded the palm to the South for leadership in politics and war, it excelled in scholarship, authorship, science and invention.

THE MIDDLE COLONIES

Between New England and the South lie the 'Empire State' of New York and the 'Keystone State' of Pennsylvania, as well as the smaller states of New Jersey and Delaware. They had certain important advantages over the other colonies. New England had little mineral wealth, no great rivers, and a cold climate. As John Greenleaf Whittier said, 'Her yellow sands are sands alone,/Her only mines are ice and stone.' The South had a warm climate and great rivers, but it lay further away from England.

Pennsylvania had hidden treasures of oil and coal. New York had the only easy passage from the Atlantic coast to the Great Lakes by way of the Hudson and Mohawk Rivers and, in later times, the Erie Canal. The Hudson was not so much a river as a 'drowned valley,' vast in extent, and opening on one of the best harbors in the world. The climate of these Middle Colonies was midway between the sternness of New England and the relaxing heat of the South.

Another characteristic of the Middle Colonies was the cosmopolitan character of its population. New York was Dutch before it became English; Delaware was originally a Swedish settlement; Pennsylvania, because of its religious tolerance, attracted many dissidents from Germany, and some of these Mennonites cling to this day to their German speech and Old World customs. In more recent years, immigrants have poured into the mines and factories of Pennsylvania, and today New York has more Jews than Jerusalem, more Irish than Dublin, and more Blacks than any African city. It also has large contingents of a dozen other peoples.

The Dutch West Indies Company established the first settlements on Manhattan Island, purchased from the Indians in 1626, and the colony remained Dutch until 1664. It extended north to Albany, incorporated much of New Jersey and took over a small Swedish settlement in Delaware.

Opposite top: In 1661 William Penn signed a treaty with the Indians and founded the Province of Pennsylvania. The illustration of the signing is by Currier and Ives. *Opposite below:* The Dutch settlers in the Middle Colonies did a great deal of trading with the local Indians. *Top left:* One of the most distinguished of all Americans was the Renaissance Man from Pennsylvania (although he was born in Massachusetts) – Benjamin Franklin. *Top right:* An engraving of the Philadelphia State House by William Birch and Son shows what the structure looked like in 1798 – 10 years after the United States Constitution was ratified. *Above:* Benjamin Franklin and his kite experiment. Although scientists say that Franklin was lucky in not being electrocuted, he did prove that lightning was a form of electricity – a fact that had been unknown before he began his scientific research.

Many old American families trace their family trees back to these 'Knickerbocker Dutch' origins. After a war between Britain and the Netherlands, New Netherland became New York and New Amsterdam, New York City (both named for the Duke of York).

The Dutch element in the present American population is not very large, but it contains some famous names, such as the two Presidents Roosevelt, and several wealthy landlords and financiers. In colonial times New York lagged behind Virginia, Massachusetts and Pennsylvania in population, but under the republic it grew rapidly. New York City is still the most populous city, and New York State is second in population only to California.

King Charles II owed a debt to Admiral Sir William Penn. It was not convenient for him to pay it in cash, but it could be paid in land. Penn's son, William Penn, was a 'Friend,' or Quaker, who wanted a home for his persecuted fellow believers. He suggested the appropriate name 'Sylvania' (the land of woods) for the colony. Charles clapped 'Penn' onto this, and it became Pennsylvania. Penn then bought the land from the Indians – a transaction of which Voltaire later said, with a slight exaggeration, 'It was the only treaty not confirmed by oaths, and the only one not broken by either side.'

Pennsylvania prospered greatly, although there was some friction between the 'proprietors,' the descendents of Penn, and the settlers. The chief city was Philadelphia, or 'The City of Brotherly Love,' which became for a time the chief city in the colonies.

The most important Pennsylvanian, very probably the most important American in the whole colonial period, was Benjamin Franklin. He was born in Boston, as New Englanders love to point out, but his entire career was wrapped up in Pennsylvania. He has been called 'the most typical American' and 'the only man who never bored anyone.' Certainly few, if any, men have been more versatile. He was printer, publisher, author, postmaster, diplomat, statesman and natural scientist. In this last capacity he was most widely known for experiments proving that lightning was a form of electricity. He also took the temperature of ocean currents, interested himself in agriculture, medicine and geology and invented the 'Franklin Stove.'

He suggested, although he was unable to realize, a federation of the 13 colonies. As ambassador to France, he helped bring about the alliance with the rebel colonies which determined the result of the Revolution. He gave his approval to the new Constitution.

The French thought of him as Jean Jacques Rousseau's 'natural man,' unspoiled by civilization. As a matter of fact, he was as much at home in Paris as in Philadelphia. Yet there remained in him some trace of the original canny 'Poor Richard,' who gave a library to a town that had asked for a bell: 'Sense being preferable to sound,' and suggested the turkey as a better American emblem than the eagle since it was native to America and a 'more useful bird.'

AMERICA: FRENCH OR BRITISH?

From the revolution of 1688 which brought the Dutch *stadhouder* (head of state) to the British throne as King William III, to the Battle of Waterloo in 1815, there was a succession of wars to curb the ambitious power of France. Three things were at stake: Europe, India and North America. Sometimes it is hard to tell whether there was a European conflict which spread to the colonies or a colonial struggle which spread to Europe.

Some historians have termed this the 'Second Hundred Years' War with France.' Of course, there were long periods of peace between wars, but neither was the first Hundred Years' War continuous. The real difference was that, in the 14th century, English kings were striving to make good their title to rule France. In the 18th century, no one thought of such a conquest. It was, rather, so far as the British were concerned, a conflict to determine whether French or British colonial imperialism should predominate. The colonists, instead of using European names, usually referred to each war by the name of the monarch then ruling. Thus the War of the League of Augsburg became 'King William's War'; the War of the Spanish Succession, 'Queen Anne's War.' The War of the Austrian Succession became 'King George's War.' The Seven Years' War, however, became the 'French and Indian War,' because the Indian allies of the French seemed almost as great a danger as the French themselves.

These were not 'total wars' like the two World Wars, but rather wars with limited objectives, frequently ending in a compromise, and sometimes in a shift of alliances. The ally of yesterday might be the enemy of tomorrow. But at no time during this period were France and Britain anything but hostile.

The French had certain advantages. They had the larger home population, a stronger army, a centralized command and the friendship of more Indian tribes. But the British assets were, in the long run, more important. Sea power was theirs, and colonies could be reinforced only by sea. Though the French Empire in America was more extensive, it had a much smaller population. It was bureaucratically managed and the men on the spot were poorly supported, in India and America alike. France was a continental country and had at all times to defend her European frontiers, whereas the British, secure behind their fleet, could concentrate on colonies, commerce, and shipping – both mercantile and naval.

By the time of the Treaty of Utrecht (1713) the British controlled Acadia, which they renamed Nova Scotia, and expelled many of the French inhabitants, some of whom reappeared in French Louisiana as 'Cajuns.' But there was no culmination until the French and Indian War (1756–63). Early in that struggle, the English commander, Edward Braddock, fell into an Indian ambush. George Washington, in charge of

Above: French-Canadian soldiers were often equipped with snowshoes in order to traverse the winter landscapes. *Left:* An engraving made by Thomas Johnston showing 'Quebec, The Capital of New-France, a Bishopric, and Seat of the Soverain Court.' In the foreground is the St Lawrence River. In the distance at the far left is the Citadel, which exists today. The scene shows both the Upper and Lower Town. At the far left in the Upper Town is the Castle. The Cathedral of Our Lady is the building with the highest tower, and the bishop's house is down the hill directly in front of the cathedral. *Top right:* One of the decisive battles of the French and Indian War was the defeat of the British commander, Gen Edward Braddock. *Bottom right:* An early British thrust into Canada was the taking of Louisburg, on Cape Breton Island in Canada in 1745. Here the British Forces of New England are being landed.

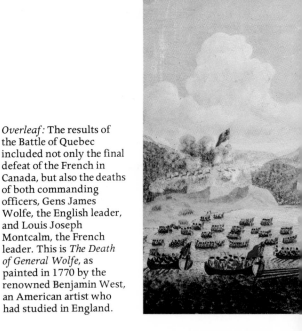

Overleaf: The results of the Battle of Quebec included not only the final defeat of the French in Canada, but also the deaths of both commanding officers, Gens James Wolfe, the English leader, and Louis Joseph Montcalm, the French leader. This is *The Death of General Wolfe*, as painted in 1770 by the renowned Benjamin West, an American artist who had studied in England.

the American militia, succeeded with difficulty in saving some remnants from the defeat. But the war as a whole went in favor of the British. General James Wolfe sailed past Quebec, climbed the steep banks of the St Lawrence, and defeated the French commander, Louis Joseph Montcalm. The fall of Quebec virtually ended the American phase of that war. The British fleet prevented any relief to 'New France.'

The Peace of Paris (1763) gave French Canada to Britain. It also virtually ended Marquis Joseph François Dupleix's hope of a French Empire in India, leaving Robert Clive triumphant. A coincident treaty at Huburtus-burg signalled the victory of Frederick the Great of Prussia over Maria Theresa of Austria. Seldom has a peace settlement been more decisive or more gratifying to the victors.

But some observers were intelligent enough to see that in the very completeness of her victory, Britain had imperilled her hold on the American mainland colonies. What need had the American colonists of a 'mother country' now? The Spaniards were weak and far away; the Americans, from long experience, understood Indian warfare better than did the British regulars. France had been their sole dread, and this had been removed. This would not, of itself, have meant secession; Canada, New Zealand and Australia remain content within the British Commonwealth of Nations today. But it required very intelligent and systematic handling affairs to keep the 13 colonies loyal to Crown and Empire.

THE EMERGENCE OF AMERICAN NATIONALITY

How did the people of the 13 colonies come to think of themselves as 'Americans' rather than as transplanted Englishmen? One cause was sheer distance. The Atlantic was a far more formidable barrier in the days of sailing ships than in the times of the 19th century steamer or the 20th century airplane. Although traffic was incessant, the trip took weeks. This had a two-fold result. It forced the colonists back on their own resources and it caused the British government always to be late in dealing with colonial affairs. During the Revolution, by the time local officials could get in touch with the home government and the government could send out instructions, the situation might have so changed as to make those instructions completely out of date.

Another cause was that the American population, though mainly English, contained immigrants from other countries. As Thomas Paine put it, America was the child of Europe, not of England only. A French immigrant, St Jean de Crèvecoeur, in his *Letters from an American Farmer* (1782), asked and answered the question, 'Whence come these people?'

'They are a mixture of English, Scotch, Irish, French, Dutch, Germans and Swedes . . . Here individuals of all nations are melted into a new race of men, whose labours and posterity will one day cause great changes in the world.' But probably the most important cause of all was neither physical distance nor ethnic variety, but the conditions of frontier life.

This life style forced on the Americans a greater simplicity of social and economic life than prevailed in Europe. There was little abject poverty, but no great fortunes, and practically no leisure class, for the southern planters were kept busy managing their estates and looking after their slaves; and the northern aristocracy, so far as there was any, consisted of busy merchants and lawyers. The great bulk of the population were farmers who had to do almost everything for themselves.

An intelligent German traveler, Johann Schoepf, in his *Travels in the Confederation, 1783–84*, mentions a quotation from an American of the time: 'I am a weaver, shoemaker, farrier, wheelwright, farmer, gardener and, when it can't be helped, a soldier. I bake my bread, brew my beer, kill my pigs; I grind my axe and knives; I built those stalls and that shed there; I am barber, leech and doctor.'

Schoepf pointed out that 'The man was everything at no expense for a

Above left: The French-born essayist, Hector St John de Crèvecoeur, declared that 'there is room for everybody in America,' a land he referred to as 'this smiling country.' *Above right:* A French engraving praising Thomas Paine for being 'Secretary of the Congress in the Department of Foreign Affairs, during the War of America, author of *Common Sense* and *The Replies to Burke*. Deputy to the National Convention for the Department of Pas de Calais, the first year of the Republic.' *Below left:* Americans of the time were busy people, if one can believe this illustration from Benjamin Franklin's *Poor Richard's Almanac. Opposite top:* One of the earliest industries in the colonies was the manufacture of beaver hats, and this shows the final ironing process. *Below:* A summer scene on a small prosperous farm near Batavia, New York.

license, and could do anything, as indeed his countrymen in America generally can.'

This versatility was necessary in a pioneer environment, and it obviously had many advantages, but there were some drawbacks, too. In the early days of the republic it led to the belief that 'anybody can teach school,' and 'anybody can fill a public office.' It also fostered the idea that successful generals were by that fact good material for presidents, which might or might not be the case.

One reason for the absence of extreme poverty was the possibility of gaining land on easy terms. Some laborers came over as 'indentured servants,' paying for their passage by promising to work a certain number of years. But once free of their indentures, they did not sink into a landless proletariat or even become tenant farmers. As a rule they moved west to new ground and set up for themselves.

Since the entire East was wooded, nearly all private homes were built of wood. But recent research has shown that the 'log cabin' was originally devised by Swedish immigrants; the English settlers in both Virginia and New England made frame houses. Eventually, however, the log cabin became common in the frontier settlements as the cheapest and most easily constructed type of dwelling.

In the older settlements near the Atlantic coast, some public buildings were of brick or stone, and some of the wealthier plantation homes in the South had fine linen, glass and chinaware, silverware imported from England and family portraits. But the stateliest American homes did not rival the European mansions of the wealthy.

THE REBELLIOUS DAUGHTERS

Originally, there had been in America three types of colonies: those planted by a chartered company, as in Virginia and Massachusetts; those with individual proprietor, as in Pennsylvania, Maryland and Georgia; and the royal, as in New York. But eventually they tended to the same pattern; the rights of chartered companies and of individual proprietors yielded to the claims of the Crown.

The general system consisted of a governor, appointed by Britain, and a two-house legislature, of which the lower one was elected by the voters of the colony, the upper house being appointed. Although there was usually a property qualification for the suffrage, it was easier to become a landowner in any of the 13 colonies than it was in Great Britain, and so the colonists, in certain respects, really enjoyed a greater degree of popular self-government than the majority of English, Scottish or Irish.

But there is always a possibility of friction between an executive chosen in one fashion and a legislature chosen in another. Although the colonies had 'representative' government, they did not, like the British Dominions today, enjoy 'responsible' government. Dissension between royal governors and popular legislature was more the rule than the exception. Moreover, the governors were not selected for their knowledge of American conditions or their sympathy with the Americans; they represented family favor or expediency in British politics.

In three specific areas conflict between the colonists and the mother country was most acute: commerce, taxation and the settlement of western lands. The British generally regarded the colonies as 'plantations' established in the interest of British commerce; 'governing,' as Arthur Young put it, 'great nations on the maxims of the counter.' In theory, the colonists recognized the right of the British government to regulate foreign trade; but the manner in which this was done irked them extremely. They especially resented not being able to trade directly with the French, Spanish and Dutch colonies in the West Indies. Hence there was a good deal of smuggling. In Europe, as well as in America, smuggling was common; boats of light draft could easily find harbor, and popular opinion was more often with the smuggler, who made goods cheaper, than with the law enforcement officers.

The matter of taxation was more serious. The French and Indian war had been expensive and British opinion was that the colonists should bear their share of the expense since they had reaped so much advantage from the removal of the French from their neighborhood. But how to exact revenue from the penny-pinching colonial legislatures? The first device was the Stamp Act. This was not a postage matter – it was the imposition of an official stamp duty on legal papers. It encountered general resistance. The Stamp Act was withdrawn, but the government laid special duties on a variety of commodities which could be represented as merely commercial regulation, although their purpose was to raise revenue.

Many of these duties were dropped, but a duty on tea remained, partly to aid the East India Company and partly to maintain the right of the British Parliament to tax the colonies.

The British theory was that the authority of Parliament was coextensive with the Empire. To be sure, the colonists had no representation in Parliament, but they were 'virtually' represented by the House of Commons. The Americans held that their colonial legislature had the sole right to levy taxes. Which theory was the sounder in law was debatable. but the American view was closer to the realities of the situation. To contend that a man in New York was represented by a voter in Yorkshire, merely because both were commoners and British subjects, was stretching abstract theory to the breaking point.

After acquiring French Canada, the British government, by the Quebec Act of 1774, extended the frontier as far as the Ohio River, thus cancelling the charter claims of several colonies, notably Virginia, Mas-

sachusetts and Connecticut. This act left the French their civil law, but provided no representation for the people. With regard to the French it was a wise measure; the people of Quebec were attached to their language and their Roman Catholic Church. They had never enjoyed representative government, and the British criminal law, now introduced, was milder than the French. But it also meant that an English settler beyond the mountains would find himself unrepresented and in a province dominated by the French language and the Roman faith.

In none of these measures did the British government intend injustice or tyranny. The right to regulate trade was traditional; the tax devices were mainly to cover the expenses of the recent war with France; and the restrictions on western settlement were partly to conciliate the people of Quebec and partly to avoid wars with the Indian tribes. The whole trouble was that measures which seemed just and reasonable in London might look different to a Virginia planter, a Boston merchant or a frontier farmer in western Pennsylvania.

Some of the better-informed British statesmen pointed this out to Parliament – among them William Pitt, the Earl of Chatham; Edmund Burke, the Irish orator; and Charles Fox, the liberal Whig leader. But King George III was an obstinate man, Lord North and his ministry followed the royal lead, and the majority of the members of Parliament knew little and cared less about colonial opinion.

As is often the case, war broke out over a minor incident. Resentful of the tea duty, a party of patriots, disguised as Indians, dumped a load of tea into Boston Harbor. The British government responded with severe punishment. They temporarily closed the port of Boston, suspended the Charter of Massachusetts, authorized the quartering troops in private homes and provided that military offenses against civilians should be tried outside the colony. These 'Intolerable Acts' (as the patriots called them) provoked the first armed resistance.

Opposite top: The Americans protested the Stamp Act and people in Boston even went so far as to burn the papers that had been sent from England in 1764. *Opposite bottom:* King George III of England, the monarch at the time of the American Revolution. *Top:* The Boston Tea Party was the event in which Americans dressed as Indians threw the cargoes of the English tea ships into Boston

Harbor 16 December 1773. *Above:* The Boston Massacre. On 5 March 1770 a jeering crowd of men and boys were teasing a British sentry. He was joined by seven soldiers and their commander. The jeering continued and the soldiers fired into the crowd, killing three and mortally wounding two others.

Opposite top: Minute Men being summoned from their homes to fight. Men such as these fought the British in the Battles of Lexington and Concord 19 April 1775. *Opposite far left:* British troops march through the town of Concord prior to the battle, while Col Francis Smith and Maj John Pitcairn reconnoiter the area from the cemetery. *Bottom left:* British troops marching back from Lexington to their headquarters in Boston and being harassed by the expert snipers of the Minute Men. *Above:* John Trumbull painted *The Battle of Bunker Hill.* On 17 June 1775 the British were sent to occupy Breed's Hill to prevent the Americans from using it as a site for their cannons to bombard Boston, which was occupied by the British. The battle has mistakenly been named after nearby Bunker Hill. *Right:* Another view of the battle. *Overleaf:* Raising the Liberty Pole, 1776.

GEORGE WASHINGTON

The first British miscalculation was that the war could be confined to Massachusetts. But already the colony was in touch with other colonies by 'committees of correspondence'. Militia were being organized everywhere. The first battles, naturally, were fought in the neighborhood of Boston – Lexington, Concord and Bunker Hill. But when the colonists sought a commander-in-chief, they looked to Virginia.

George Washington (1732–99) was no revolutionary firebrand like Samuel Adams, Patrick Henry or Tom Paine. He was a well-to-do planter, rather conservative by temperament, a vestryman of the Episcopal Church and a sometime member of the Virginia House of Burgesses. He had a good military record in the French and Indian War, where he extricated the remnant of Braddock's army from defeat.

But, interested as he was in his profession of arms, always nearest to his heart was his estate of Mount Vernon. King George III was often affectionately called 'Farmer George' by his subjects, and the same title might be given to his famous rival. Whenever relieved of political or military duty, he returned to his plantation. Here he was happiest and most at home.

Was he a great general in the European sense? It is impossible to say, for at no time did he have a very large or well-disciplined army. His troops, like himself, were nine parts farmer to one part soldier. But he had the qualities needed for welding a mass of raw volunteers into an efficient force and keeping a spirit of constant resolution among his troops.

Washington himself was a strict, even a stern, disciplinarian, ready to dismiss an inefficient officer or order flogging for a deserter. Some experienced foreign officers brought stiffening to the ranks – the Marquis de Lafayette from France, Baron von Steuben from Germany, Taddeus Kosciusko from Poland. But the task before the rebel forces was almost an impossible one. The Americans were in the position of a man simultaneously building a shop, doing business in it and putting out a fire threatening to consume it. An army had to be improvised, a new government created and a war successfully prosecuted.

On the face of the matter the British should have won easily. They had the support of a wealthy and respectable section of the population who called themselves 'Loyalists,' and whom the other called 'Tories;' they had the support of trained veteran British soldiers; they had the aid of mercenaries from Hanover and Hesse and the support of certain Indian tribes.

Their opponents, the 'Patriots' to themselves and 'Rebels' to the British, probably outnumbered the Loyalists and were excellent raw material for warfare. They usually knew how to shoot, ride and take care of themselves in the open. But after a victory they were hard to hold in line, desiring to get back to their neglected farms. In the later stages of the war they had effective support from France.

There was, as always in revolutions, a third party, which tends to get overlooked – the neutral who wished to get ahead with the spring plowing under whatever flag. They were especially numerous among the non-British elements in the population, such as the Germans and the Dutch. Many Quakers also, believing that all war was contrary to Christian teaching, refrained from taking either side.

Fortunately for the American cause, the British, with far less excuse, were equally inefficient. The vast wildernesses of America, the unbroken forests, the scattered farms, were an unfamiliar terrain to British soldiers accustomed to win wars by pitched battles and captured cities. The British had their share of victories and occupied the larger towns, but found themselves as far as ever from conquering America.

The British had some able generals, but some of these were half-hearted, feeling that the colonists had some right on their side, and some were too easy-going, believing the revolution a mere flash in the pan,

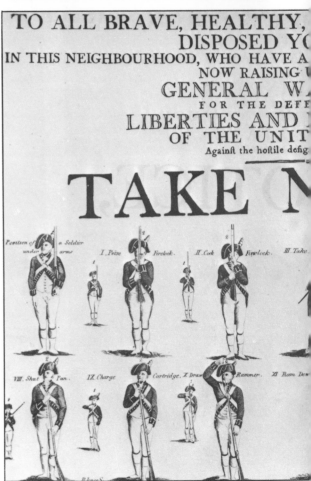

Top: George Washington at the age of 40 – three years before he was appointed Commander of the Army. *Above:* A printed call to enlist in the Continental Army. Enlistees were offered 'a bounty of twelve dollars, an annual and fully sufficient supply of good and handsome cloathing, a daily allowance of a large and ample ration of provisions, together with sixty dollars a year in gold and silver money on account of pay . . .'. *Top*

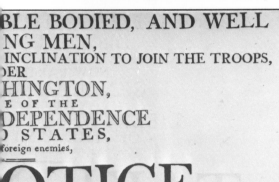

left: A portrait of George Washington at Yorktown. *Above right:* A map of George Washington's position on the York River in 1781. On 19 October 1781, Gen Charles Cornwallis surrendered his entire command at Yorktown. This combined French and American victory practically assured the independence of the United States.

soon to be extinguished. The direction of the war from London was most incompetent. The Colonial Secretary, Lord George Germain, had been dismissed from the army as 'unfit to serve in any military capacity,' and the Earl of Sandwich, First Lord of the Admiralty, has been termed by a historian who himself filled the naval office, 'the most negligent administrator who ever sat at the head of the table at the Admiralty.' King George had zeal but little wisdom to contribute to the war, and his chief minister, Lord North, followed his lead, but with increasing reluctance, for he could see that the war was going badly.

Washington, as his best biographer, Douglas Freeman, has stated, 'could war the better against Britain because he was not at war with himself. None of his energies had to be diverted from administration and planning and operations to combat selfish ambition or to overcome distracting passions.'

THE REVOLUTION AS A CIVIL WAR

The task of the British was to occupy Boston, New York, Philadelphia (where the Continental Congress met) and Charleston; to seal off New England from the rest of the colonies by an expedition based in Canada; and to use their fleet to land forces from Europe wherever they might be needed. They drove Washington's forces from Long Island into Manhattan and thence to New Jersey and Pennsylvania. Washington did his best to delay the British advance, but eventually he was forced into winter quarters in Valley Forge, Pennsylvania.

His troops were ill-supplied with food and clothing and the long series of retreats was discouraging. One acid British critic said, 'Any general but [William] Howe could have beaten Washington, and any general but Washington could have beaten Howe.' This may have been an underestimation of Washington, since he made an unexpected attack on the Hessians in Trenton who were celebrating the Christmas of 1776.

General John Burgoyne planned to move south from Canada and effect a juncture with Howe's forces moving north. But Howe, receiving contradictory instructions from the Colonial Office, took time out to seize Philadelphia, and Burgoyne, unsupported, was defeated by General Gates at Saratoga in 1777. This has been generally considered the decisive turning point in the war, since it caused France to decide to throw in her lot with the Americans.

When the war first broke out in 1775, most colonists were not thinking of independence; they were contending for 'the rights of Englishmen.' But the war itself changed their war aims. Heavy losses on both sides, allegations of atrocities (some true, some false) and the propaganda of such writers as Thomas Paine who, in his pamphlets *Common Sense* and *The Crisis*, urged that only complete independence would give security to the Americans, changed this perspective.

By the summer of 1776, the patriot forces were ready for the final step. The Continental Congress passed a resolution for independence on 2 July. Thomas Jefferson was asked to draw up a declaration, justifying this action. Two days later, this declaration was presented and that date has ever since been celebrated as a national holiday. The larger part of the

Left: The British, under the command of Cornwallis, attacked Fort Lee, New Jersey. Here they are scaling the palisades on the New Jersey side of the Hudson River. *Above:* Washington set up his winter quarters at Valley Forge near Philadelphia during the winter of 1777–78. The illustration shows Washington and Lafayette visiting the suffering soldiers. *Right:* The capture of the Hessians at Trenton, New Jersey. On 26 December 1776 Washington defied the floating ice in the Delaware River, landed above the town, and attacked the garrison of Hessian mercenary troops. The attack had been a gamble, but more than 900 prisoners were taken and the morale of the young country was revived. *Overleaf:* Another turning point in the war – the surrender of Gen John Burgoyne at Saratoga, New York. The American forces outnumbered the British, and in the second of two battles, both fought at Freeman's Farm near Saratoga, the British were defeated 17 October 1777.

Declaration of Independence consists of a listing of concrete grievances against the British Crown, some of long standing, others arising from the war itself. But the preamble, asserting the general principle of popular government, has been of the most perennial interest:

> We hold these truths to be self-evident, that all men are created equal, that they are endowed by their Creator with certain unalienable rights, that among these are life, liberty, and the pursuit of happiness. That to secure these rights governments are instituted among men, deriving their just powers from the consent of the governed, that whenever any form of government becomes destructive of these ends, it is the right of the people to alter or abolish it, and to institute new government, laying its foundations on such principles, and organizing its powers in such form, as to them shall seem most likely to effect their safety and happiness.

After this, nothing but complete national independence would satisfy the Americans, and, understandably, the British were reluctant to grant that. The war had to be fought to a definite conclusion. Any chance of compromise, conceding certain points to the colonies but keeping them within the Empire, had been lost.

THE REVOLUTION AS AN INTERNATIONAL WAR

With the French alliance, the troubles of England began to multiply. France, Spain and the Netherlands all joined against her; some of the northern nations of Europe formed an 'armed neutrality,' designed to prevent interference with their trade, and Ireland stood on the verge of rebellion. Henry Grattan proposed in the Irish Parliament that 'No power on earth but the King, Lords and Commons of Ireland, is competent to bind Ireland.' Relics of English control were swept away, and with them many of the so-called 'penal laws' against Roman Catholics. Unfortunately, the stubborn opposition of King George III prevented Roman Catholics, who constituted the majority of the Irish people, from being admitted to the Irish Parliament.

Discontent grew in England. Henry Fox, the Whig leader in the House of Commons, pronounced the war as 'unjust in its principles and as absurd in its prosecution, as it would be ruinous in its consequences.' The hopes of British victory faded when a British army under Lord Charles Cornwallis was trapped at Yorktown between Washington's troops and a French fleet and was compelled to surrender. The war still dragged on for a few months, especially in the southern colonies, but defeat could only be deferred, not averted.

It is true that the French alliance cut both ways. The Earl of Chatham (the elder William Pitt), who had championed the cause of the colonies in terms which might, in a less tolerant age or country, have led to a prosecution for treason, in his last days protested against any surrender to France. Benedict Arnold, although his personal motive in betraying the American cause was largely wounded pride and self-interest, justified it publicly by denouncing the French alliance.

Below: Betsy Ross shows 'Old Glory' to an admiring Gen Washington. *Opposite top:* A gathering of the 'Over-Mountain' men from the Watauga settlements, meeting at Sycamore Flats prior to marching against the Tories at King's Mountain, North Carolina. Their attack in October 1780 annihilated Maj Patrick Ferguson's command and delayed the British advance into North Carolina until 1781. *Opposite bottom:* The American troops lost the Battle of Monmouth, New Jersey 28 June 1778. This permitted Gen Henry Clinton to march his British troops into New York. *Overleaf:* In the Battle of Cowpens on January 1781 Banastre Tarleton's hated legion was defeated.

Battle of Cowpens 17th of January 1781.

Left: A British satirical drawing of 1778 giving reasons on why the United States should accept friendly overtures of trade from the British commissioners. Below: Gen Francis Marion, the 'Swamp Fox,' entertains a British officer in his South Carolina swamp encampment. Opposite top: John Paul Jones on the Bonhomme Richard was the victor over the British Capt Pearson who commanded the Serapis. The sea battle took place 22 September 1779. Opposite bottom: The Marquis Marie Joseph Paul Yves Roch Gilbert du Motier de Lafayette – a prime mover in winning French support for the American cause, a leader in the American Army, and a hero in the French Republic.

On the other hand, most Englishmen felt that, grievous as would be the losses of 13 colonies, it might be still more damaging to prolong a costly and losing war, and perhaps encourage French hopes of regaining Canada.

In 1782 the Tory ministry of Lord North resigned, and the Whigs under Shelburne consented to negotiate peace. In 1783 the final settlement was made. Not only was the United States to be independent, but its boundaries were to be extended to the Mississippi River. Florida, which for 20 years had been British, went back to Spain. France gained little except the satisfaction of defeating her chief adversary, for the British navy was still supreme. Loyalists who had lost their property by confiscation were to be reimbursed; but the failure of the legislatures to act and the inability of the national government to compel action largely nullified this stipulation. Eventually the British settled the more intransigent Tories in upper Canada (Ontario) under the name of 'United Empire Loyalists.'

The American Revolution had a greater effect on France than on Britain. It was one more war than the French treasury could afford, and led to national bankruptcy and the calling of the national legislature (the *Estates General*) which started the French Revolution. Moreover, some liberal idealists, such as Lafayette, were impressed by seeing at first hand the creation of a popular government on a large scale. Why not for France as well?

The revolution ended King George's attempt at personal government. It is true that the younger William Pitt revived the Tory Party and, in the main, pleased the king. But his policies were his own – not, as had been the case of Bute and North, a mere echo of the king's.

PART 2
THE YOUNG REPUBLIC, 1784-1865

Three things are particularly worth noting during this period: the making of a workable constitution; the westward movement; and the growing division between North and South, chiefly over the slavery question.

Without the ratification of the Constitution, the American experiment might well have failed. The Revolutionary Articles of Confederation hardly amounted to more than an alliance of 13 sovereign states. A more permanent structure was essential to prevent the breakup of the Union.

The westward movement had a double importance. Of course it meant the subjugation of the wilderness and the defeat of Indian tribes. Populous and prosperous cities grew where once there had been almost unbroken forest. But it also meant a reciprocal influence of the pioneer West on the more conservative East. With Andrew Jackson, it became common to pick western presidents. As frontier conditions promoted democracy, not only political life, but also social life became more democratic. The cult of the 'common man' was added to the national tradition.

One institution, however, was the reverse of democratic. This was slavery. For climatic reasons this became a sectional issue. Only in the South was cheap plantation labor profitable. At first, the South was as nationalistic as any part of the country, but eventually the South found itself outnumbered and its 'peculiar institution' of slavery endangered. This led southern leaders to fall back on 'state sovereignty' and, at the election of Abraham Lincoln as an anti-slavery president, to secede.

The ensuing Civil War was the great watershed across American history. Out of a population, North and South, of barely 30 million, it enlisted 10 per cent, killed (in battle or by disease) some 400,000, crippled other thousands for life, put the North and the Republican Party in power for a generation and transformed a mainly agricultural country into a mainly industrial and commercial one. Almost incidentally, it made 4 million slaves freedmen.

The Emigrant Train
Bedding Down for the
Night.

MAKING THE CONSTITUTION

Alexander Hamilton laid a very precise finger on the chief defect of the Articles of Confederation:

> We may indeed be said to have reached almost the last stage of national humiliation . . . The great and radical vice in the construction of the existing Confederation is the principle of legislation for States or Governments, in their corporate or collective capacities, as contradistinguished from the individuals of which they consist . . . The United States has an indefinite discretion to make requisitions, for men and money; but they have no authority to raise either, by regulations extending to the individual citizens . . . though in theory their resolutions concerning these objects are laws, constitutionally binding on the members of the Union, yet in practice they are merely recommendations which the States observe or disregard at their option.

More briefly stated, the national Congress had legislative power, but no executive power. That belonged to the states.

For example, the peace had provided that Loyalists who had been deprived of their property should be reimbursed. Congress recommended that the states do this; but some of them failed to do so, which gave the British an excuse for holding on to certain forts in the Northwest, which by treaty should have reverted to the United States.

There were other difficulties. One was the danger that some states might enact tariffs against the rest; or, swept by a radical impulse, might deny the obligation of contracts, repudiate public or private debts, and issue inflated currency.

Below: A cartoon and poem from *The Centinel*, a Massachusetts newspaper. Dated 2 August 1788 it urged the two states that had not ratified the Constitution to do so.

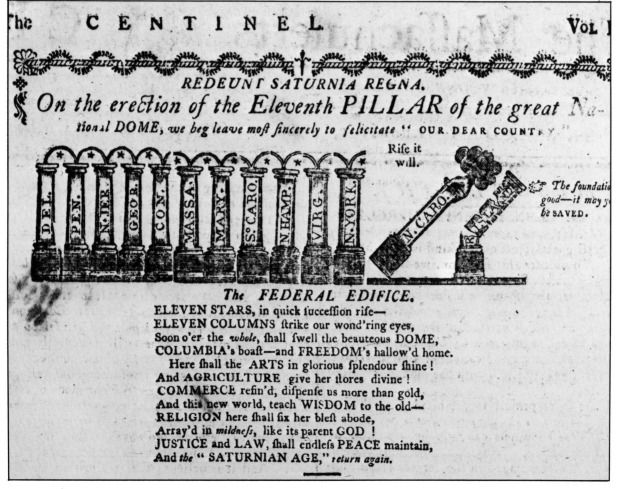

Opposite top: The signing of the Constitution in Philadelphia, 1787. George Washington had retired to Mount Vernon, his estate in Virginia, in 1783, after the war. When the Constitutional Convention gathered in 1787, he was pressed into national service again as head of the Virginia delegation, and was promptly elected president of the convention. *Opposite bottom:* Alexander Hamilton, the first Secretary of the Treasury, who established the national credit on a firm basis, made use of the taxing power of the nation, and created a banking system.

One great forward step was made before the Constitution was ratified: settling the territorial claims of certain seaboard states, especially Virginia, Massachusetts and Connecticut, to land beyond the Appalachians. The British disregard of these rights under colonial charters had been one cause of the revolution, and now the question arose in a new form. States without charter claims were jealous of those who had them; moreover, these claims at times overlapped and conflicted. A very sensible solution was reached. The new states with western claims were induced to release them, after conceding certain settlement rights to their veterans of the Revolutionary War. The whole Northwest, between the Ohio River and the Great Lakes, became territories of the nation; slavery was forbidden and certain lands set aside for schools. Territories were encouraged to hope that, when their population was large enough, Congress would permit them to organize as states, equal in rights with the original 13.

Territories were also founded in the Southwest, with the significant difference that there was no prohibition of slavery. Apart from the original 13, nearly all states had a previous existence as territories with appointed governors, but local legislatures. There were some exceptions: Maine was carved out of Massachusetts; Kentucky and West Virgina from Virgina;

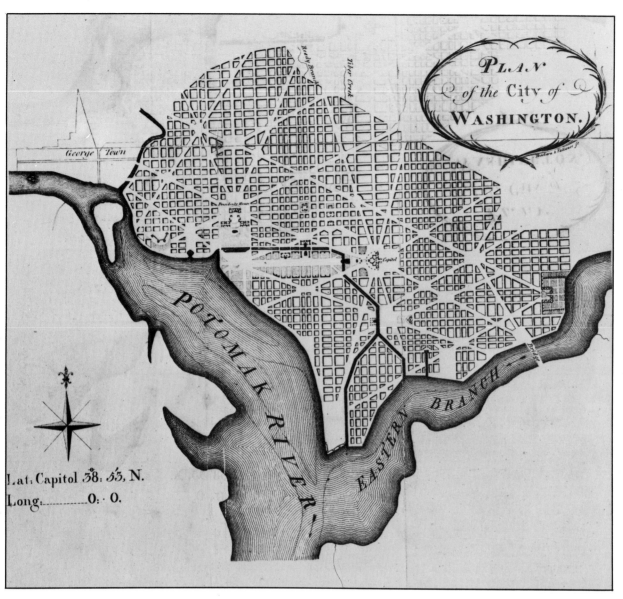

Vermont from land disputed by New York and New Hampshire; and Texas was originally an independent republic.

At first it was considered sufficient to amend the Articles of Confederation, granting increased powers to the federal government, but when the Constitutional Convention finally met, it took matters into its own hands and decided to make an entirely new Constitution to go into effect when ratified by nine of the 13 states.

The convention met privately and as a small, businesslike body. Most of its members had had some previous experience. They knew that, to make a Constitution at all, there would have to be compromises. The resulting instrument was not, perhaps, what any one of the delegates would have made if left to himself, and it has been amended many times. But it was *real*, not, like so many constitutions, a mere scrap of paper.

The chief compromise was between the larger states and the less populous ones. Congress was divided into two parts: a House of Representatives, based upon population, and a Senate, in which each state was entitled to two senators. There was to be a president, elected for four years by a special electoral college and a federal judiciary. The slave states were given a compromise in the number of representatives and presidential electors – slaves would count for 3/5 of a free man, and the slave trade with Africa was not to be forbidden until 1808.

Thomas Jefferson, who was abroad on a mission to France, liked the Constitution in general, but he and others pointed out the need for a Bill of Rights, specifying in detail the rights of individual citizens. These were speedily adopted and formed the first ten amendments. They include freedom of speech and of the press, freedom of religious worship and

Opposite top: The plan of the city of Washington in the District of Columbia. The district was established by Congress in 1790–91 and it was George Washington who selected the exact site for the 'Federal City.' The capitol for the United States was moved from Philadelphia to Washington in 1800 and Thomas Jefferson was the first president to be inaugurated in the new city. *Opposite bottom:* *The Federalist No 1*, from the New York *Independent Journal* of 27 October 1787. These articles were writings in defense of the Constitution made anonymously by Alexander Hamilton, James Madison, and John Jay. Later they were collected and published in a book entitled *The Federalist*. They still constitute the best commentary available on the Constitution as the framers intended it to be interpreted. *Above:* The chambers of the House of Representatives in Philadelphia where John Adams presented the Bill of Rights 23 September 1789.

guarantees against arbitrary arrest and punishment.

The real difficulty was not in making a Constitution, but in getting it ratified. Some states, such as Delaware and Pennsylvania, approved it quickly, but others hung in doubt. The fight was especially keen in Virginia, Massachusetts and New York. A Union from which any of these was absent would be scarcely conceivable. So James Madison of Virginia and Alexander Hamilton of New York wrote a series of able state papers (*The Federalist*) explaining and defending the new Constitution.

Hamilton would personally have liked a far more centralized government, but he championed the Constitution as the best then obtainable. Finally, all but North Carolina and Rhode Island had ratified it. Their position was now insecure, so they soon joined as well, and all 13 states were bound by its terms.

Another compromise, not directly a part of the Constitution, was on the location of the new national capital. Philadelphia, in the North, had served during the first days of the republic. Hamilton wanted state debts to be taken over by the national government. To secure this he agreed to move the capital to a southern location, between Maryland and Virgina, on the Potomac River. Here, an independent district, the District of Columbia, was established, and the capital was named after George Washington.

At first the national flag was to have a new star and a new stripe for each state. But soon the states became inconveniently numerous and the stripes began to resemble a barber's pole, so it was finally decided to have a new star for each new state but keep the 13 stripes in honor of the original 13 states.

THE FEDERALIST PERIOD: WASHINGTON AND ADAMS

President Washington was an inevitable choice. He was the only president chosen unanimously by the electoral college and the only one who did not claim the allegiance of any party. It is true that almost from the first party divisions appeared, but Washington took care to include the leaders of both factions in his first cabinet; he made Jefferson his Secretary of State and Hamilton his Secretary of the Treasury. It was very fortunate that the country had the services of this large-minded patriot as its first president, since he gave to the office traditions of dignity and civic rectitude.

Among the 'Founding Fathers' some were more brilliant: the financier Hamilton; the liberal reformer, Jefferson; the chief architect of the Constitution, Madison; the learned jurist, John Marshall and the aged patriarch, Franklin. But had any of these been chosen, partisanship would have begun immediately.

Not even Washington could stave it off indefinitely. The French Revolution of 1789–99 provoked a keen partisanship in foreign policy. France, unlike the United States, had a burden of feudal privilege to cast off. As the principal state of Continental Europe, her revolution was bound to create repercussions elsewhere. From 1792 to 1815 there was an overlapping succession of European wars, centering on France. Some Americans wanted the United States to aid France, the friend and ally of the revolution; others still had a lingering sympathy with Britain, the mother country, and, moreover, were horrified at the excesses of the French 'Reign of Terror.' The first presidents Washington, John Adams and Thomas Jefferson, all desired to keep the United States neutral, fearing the effect of another war on a country which had so recently experienced the strain of the revolution.

A treaty with England, negotiated by John Jay, was widely unpopular; it was felt to be to the advantage of the British. Although Washington was elected to a second term without opposition, criticism of his administra-

Below: Many Americans were upset with John Jay's treaty with England Dissidents burned him in effigy in 1894. *Bottom:* There was no doubt that President Washington was one of the most popular American heroes of the time. *Opposite top:* President Washington is shown with his Cabinet. *Opposite bottom:* Washington reviewing the Western Army at Fort Cumberland, Md.

tion began to appear in the press. Jefferson eventually left the cabinet. Even though Washington did not belong to the Federalist Party, the conservative party of Hamilton, they claimed him. Washington, whose chief fault was his sensitivity, complained that he had been 'abused worse than a pickpocket.' He refused a third term, and thus started a precedent, never successfully broken until Franklin Roosevelt's third term in 1940.

John Adams of Massachusetts was an avowed Federalist. During his term of office extreme partisans pushed through Congress the 'alien and sedition' laws. These gave arbitrary powers to the government to deport aliens and prosecute critics of the government for 'sedition.' Jefferson and Madison replied with resolutions in the Virginia and Kentucky legislatures denying the validity of laws so unconstitutional, and called on the states to resist them. Their aim, to vindicate freedom, was admirable, but unfortunately the attempt to make the states judges of the constitutionality of national laws created a dangerous precedent.

Yet Adams, though his sympathies were more British than French, resisted Federalist pressure to take advantage of a blunder of the French, who demanded bribes to renew diplomatic relations with the United States. The country resounded with the cry, 'Millions for defense, but not one cent for tribute!' But the president resumed negotiations when France offered more reasonable terms, and war was averted. This incident is known as the 'XYZ Affair' from the initials hiding the identity of the greedy French negotiators.

Adams, an honest and able man, had few of the qualities of the succesful politician. He was tactless and quarrelsome. But he was the progenitor of the most remarkable political family in American history. The family includes a future president (John Quincy Adams) and many diplomats, historians and political reformers. As a group, they were ruggedly honest, independent of party regularity, able, scholarly, tactless, unpopular and devoted to their country. 'Remarkable men,' rhymed the poet, Stephen Vincent Benét, 'with the tart Adams quirk/And the same Adams talent for doing good work.'

Opposite top: A lithograph published 1 October 1800 showing the American merchant ship *Planter* (right) beating off a French privateer carrying 22 guns. The engagement occurred 10 July 1799. *Opposite bottom:* The second president of the United States, John Adams. *Above:* The cartoon is of Cinque-têtes (five heads) or the Paris Monster. He is asking the Americans for more money and they refuse to give it to him. The drawing illustrates the anti-French feeling in the United States following the XYZ Affair. *Right: Bonaparte in Trouble.* Napoleon is being attacked by the Russian bear and the British lion.

JEFFERSON AND THE 'REVOLUTION OF 1800'

In the election of 1800 Jefferson, the candidate of the Republican Party (not the present Republican Party, which was born in 1854), defeated Adams, the incumbent, supported by the Federalists. But an unexpected obstacle arose. The original idea of the makers of the Constitution had been to arm each elector with two ballots; the one with the highest vote to be president, the next highest, vice president. Party discipline put an end to this. All the victorious electors voted for Jefferson and Aaron Burr, most of them intending Jefferson for the higher post. But legally there was a tie and the election, according to the Constitution, went to the House of Representatives.

Some embittered Federalists wanted to support Burr in order to keep out their chief adversary, Jefferson. But Hamilton vetoed that plan. He regarded Jefferson as dangerously liberal, but honest and patriotic; Burr he considered a mere intriguer.

So Jefferson was elected and the Constitution amended to provide that the electors should vote separately for president and vice president. Never again was there a tie. But the vice president has, while the president lives, only the tame duty of presiding over the Senate. Therefore, the vice presidency ceased to be a coveted office. The party nomination for the post has often been refused, and the majority of its occupants have been rather mediocre men, chosen for a geographical balance on the party ticket, or to appease some discontented faction.

Aaron Burr was, if not the most sinister, at least the most controversial figure who ever came within reaching distance of the presidency. He killed Hamilton in a duel to avenge an insult, and he was tried in Jefferson's time for a conspiracy to erect some sort of personal empire in the West. He was acquitted, and may be entitled to the benefit of the doubt.

Top: Aaron Burr. The third vice-president of the United States, Burr later was involved in a plot to take New York and New England out of the United States. *Above:* Alexander Hamilton learned of the plot, exposed Burr, and was challenged and killed in a duel with Burr. *Left:* Thomas Jefferson preparing to depart for his inauguration in 1801. *Opposite top:* The White House in Washington DC was not always the grand edifice that it is now, as can be seen in this sketch, probably drawn in 1799. *Opposite bottom:* Alexander Hamilton was mortally wounded in his duel with Aaron Burr.

HOOPER Sc

Jefferson, conciliatory by nature, offered an olive branch to the opposing Federalists. In his inaugural address, 4 March 1801, he said:

> We are all republicans, we are all federalists . . .
> Peace, commerce and honest friendship with all nations,
> entangling alliances with none . . . the supremacy of the
> civil law over the military authority; economy in the public
> expense . . . encouragement of agriculture and of commerce
> as its handmaid.

There was little fault anyone could find with this, though some Federalists might doubt how long this dream of rural peace and plenty could hold its own amid a world in arms.

All agree that Jefferson's greatest achievement in the presidential chair was the Louisiana Purchase (1803). Napoleon had obtained the vast territory between the Mississippi River and the Rocky Mountains from Spain. He would have liked to have made this an overseas French Empire, but, as the British commanded the seas with their navy, this seemed hazardous. Jefferson had French sympathies, but he feared Napoleon's control over the mouth of that main artery of travel – the Mississippi – saying, 'If the French control New Orleans, we must marry ourselves to the British.' When Napoleon offered the whole territory for sale, Jefferson was eager to accept, although he had some characteristic scruples as to whether this lay within his constitutional powers. The price, 15 million dollars, was the best bargain the United States ever made.

His next step was worthy of that other side of Jefferson, the amateur of science. He sent the Lewis and Clark expedition to explore the new lands up to the source of the Mississippi and Missouri Rivers.

Like most two-term presidents, Jefferson found his second term more difficult than his first. The European war led to many incidents of interference with neutral commerce by both France and England. So, as a last resort to avoid war, he imposed an embargo on the export trade to any belligerent.

When President Theodore Roosevelt accused Jefferson of 'always doing what was most popular', he must have forgotten the embargo. The American shippers and sailors complained bitterly that they would rather run risks than cut off their trade altogether. Still Jefferson, following Washington's example and refusing a third term, was able to secure the election of his close friend and fellow-Virginian, James Madison, to the presidency.

Opposite top: The Louisiana Purchase – 30 April 1803. President Jefferson had sent James Monroe to France to assist the American Ambassador, Robert R. Livingston, in the purchase by the United States of the Isle of Orleans and West Florida. But Charles Maurice de Talleyrand, Napoleon's Foreign Minister, suggested that they buy the whole of Louisiana. The price was about $15 million. Left to right: Monroe, Livingston, Talleyrand. *Opposite bottom:* Meriwether Lewis, one of the leaders of the Lewis and Clark Expedition into the far Northwest. The expedition left St Louis 14 May 1804, explored to the mouth of the Columbia River, and was back in St Louis in September 1806. *Center top:* Napoleon Bonaparte's authorization for the sale of Louisiana to the United States. *Top right:* A cartoon entitled *Embargo.* The turtle symbolizes the embargo and Jefferson is encouraging it. 'Ograbme' is embargo spelled backwards. *Above:* A view of New Orleans at the time of the Purchase.

He continued to live on his estate, *Monticello*, to an advanced age, as an elder statesman of his party; and died on the same day as John Adams, 4 July 1826, the 50th anniversary of his Declaration of Independence. Characteristically, in his self-chosen epitaph he made no mention of his presidency, but claimed honor as the author of the Virginia statute of religious freedom, the Declaration of Independence and the University of Virginia, thus uniting the three enthusiasms of his life: religious liberty, political liberty, and popular education.

His party, which in Jackson's time took its modern name of the Democratic Party, remained in power for 52 of the next 60 years. The Federalists never again won the presidency; the quarrels between Adams and Hamilton, the charge of unpatriotic conduct in the War of 1812, and, above all, the reliance on 'the rich, the well-born, and the able,' in an increasing democratic atmosphere, doomed it to extinction in James Monroe's time. But the Federalists had, perhaps, some vicarious satisfaction in the adoption by the victorious Democratic Republicans, of some Federalist policies. Originally a states rights party, the Jeffersonians, long in power, came to look more indulgently on federal tariffs, federal banks, and other extensions of nationalism.

MADISON AND THE WAR OF 1812

James Madison was no warmonger, but he failed to avert the long-threatened intervention of the United States in the European war. Though the Americans had grievances against both sides, those against Britain were the more important, for three reasons. The British, commanding the seaways, were in a position to inflict more damage on commerce with the enemy than could the French; the British conscripted American sailors of British birth and the British had an apparently vulnerable colony in Canada, which some American expansionists hoped to annex.

Pressures on President Madison finally brought about the conflict. The British blundered in not removing or suspending their 'orders in council' against trade with France and with the numerous countries under French control. Madison was certainly a man of genius, but his talents lay in the law and the Constitution rather than in conducting war; Congress was too penurious in supplying the army and navy, and it might have gone hard with the country if the British had not been forced to turn their main attention to the war with Napoleon.

Even as it was, the British kept the United States out of Canada, and succeeded in occupying, and partly destroying, the national capital of Washington. This raid had another significance. Francis Scott Key, anxiously watching the siege of Baltimore from the deck of a ship, was inspired to write *The Star Spangled Banner*, which became the national anthem in the 1930s.

By sea, the Americans did fairly well, winning several victories in single combat between ships and sweeping Lake Erie free of a small British fleet. The best consolation of all was the land victory by Andrew Jackson at New Orleans, although it was fought after the peace treaty had been signed at Ghent. There was no Atlantic cable in those days, and neither side knew that the war had ended.

The treaty was a compromise, such as might end a drawn war. Nothing was said about the grievances with which the war started, and neither side gained territory or indemnity. But the results were favorable. The nation gained confidence, a peaceful boundary with Canada was eventually established and never again were Britain and the United States in conflict.

Some extreme Federalists were so opposed to 'Mr Madison's War,' as they termed it, that they considered secession in New England. But the Hartford Convention did not take this ultimate step and merely recommended some emendments to the Constitution. This dubious attitude increased the unpopularity of the dying Federalist Party.

Below: During the War of 1812, York (now Toronto) was attacked by the Americans 27 April 1813. Gen Dearborn led the successful raid on the capital of Upper Canada. The American soldiers set fire to the two houses of the provincial Parliament, which later gave the British an excuse to burn the government buildings in Washington DC.
Opposite top: Capt Oliver Hazard Perry and his men during the Battle of Lake Erie. In order to control the Great Lakes, a small fleet had been built on Lake Erie by the American Navy during the winter of 1812–13. Perry assumed command 27 March 1813. At Put-in-Bay on 10 September 1813 he found the British fleet and won the battle. It was in this conflict that Perry issued his famous settlement: 'We have met the enemy and they are ours.'
Opposite bottom: A view of the battle by Currier and Ives. Perry had left the *Lawrence* (far left) in a small boat and had raised his flag on the *Niagara* (center) shown pushing through the enemy lines.
Overleaf: The Battle of New Orleans, 8 January 1815, showing the death of the British commander, Maj Gen Sir Edward Pakenham. The American commander, Gen Andrew Jackson, faced an invading British army of 10,000 men. Although outnumbered almost three to one, the American troops, consisting mostly of Tennessee militia, won the day. The British suffered 2000 men killed, the Americans only 13.

Above: A representation of the capture of the City of Washington 24 August 1814. *Left:* The remains of the Capitol Building after it had been burned by the British. Although the British had had no trouble in routing the American militia that were to guard the capital, it was another story when they arrived at Baltimore. There, the American forces fought bravely and the attack on Ft McHenry failed. It was while the British were bombarding the fort that Francis Scott Key wrote *The Star Spangled Banner.* *Opposite top:* The Death of Capt James Lawrence on board the frigate *Chesapeake* during the encounter with the British frigate *Shannon,* 1 June 1813. Before he died in this battle off Boston Harbor, Lawrence uttered the famous words, 'Don't give up the ship.' *Opposite bottom:* Another view of the Battle of New Orleans.

MONROE AND HIS 'DOCTRINE'

The last of the 'Virginia Dynasty' was James Monroe. His two administrations (1817–25) are important for several reasons. One was the final disappearance of the Federalist Party. Monroe was re-elected in 1820 with only one electoral vote cast against him.

Another was the so-called 'Missouri Compromise.' Missouri wanted to enter the Union as a slave state; anti-slavery men opposed this. It was finally agreed to admit Missouri, but to leave free the territories north of the southern boundary of that state. Jefferson, foreseeing new quarrels over slavery, said that this controversy alarmed him 'like a firebell in the night.'

On the whole, however, Monroe's administration was marked by an ebb in partisan strife; it was called an 'Era of Good Feeling.' And the approval was quite general when he formulated, with the able assistance of John Quincy Adams, his Secretary of State, the doctrine known by his name.

To seek the origins of the Monroe Doctrine we must turn for a moment to the Old World. The Spanish colonies in continental America were in rebellion; no one denied the right of Spain to reconquer them – if she could. But this was beyond the capacity of Spain. The danger was that greater powers might intervene to crush a rebellion. France was feared in particular. So George Canning, on behalf of the British government, hinted to the Americans that a joint stand by both Britain and America might prevent this unfortunate result. Monroe took the hint, and broadened it into a general principle.

The Monroe Doctrine said, in effect, that any attempt of European powers to conquer or colonize any independent portion of the Americas would be considered by the United States 'an unfriendly act'.

This did not apply to colonies whose independence had not been recognized by the United States. Canada, for instance, was in no way affected; nor was Cuba, Spain's 'ever faithful isle,' which was later to have its own revolution. It was not a principle of international law; any

Above: The formulation of the Monroe Doctrine. Henry Clay is at the left and John Quincy Adams is seated next to him. James Monroe is standing. John C Calhoun is at the right of the door and Andrew Jackson is seated next to him.

Left: An election scene in front of the State House in Philadelphia in 1815. *Above:* James Monroe, the fifth president of the United States. *Opposite:* A slave market scene on the Gambia River on the coast of Africa. The discovery that cotton could be grown profitably by means of slave labor revived the institution of slavery just at a time when it seemed likely to disappear.

European power might disregard it, if it chose to take the risk. It was not even an American law. It was neither more nor less than a declaration of policy.

But it so chimed in with the American sentiment that no subsequent administration has departed from it, and it has been appealed to on several subsequent occasions. Prince Klemens von Metternich, Europe's arch-priest of reaction, called Canning 'a malevolent meteor,' but he did not risk a war against the combined British and American fleets. Canning, somewhat boastfully, claimed that he 'had called a New World into existence, to redress the balance of the Old!'

Since the Federalist Party had disappeared, the election of 1824 presented only Jeffersonian candidates but there were four of these: Crawford of Georgia, Henry Clay of Kentucky, Andrew Jackson from Tennessee and John Quincy Adams (the son of John Adams) from Massachusetts.

None of these gained a majority of the electoral college, and so the election went into the House of Representatives. Crawford's health eliminated him and Clay threw his strength to Adams, who won. The Jackson men were angry and hinted at a 'corrupt bargain' when Clay was later made secretary of State. Jackson had the largest popular vote of the four candidates and this should, so they said, have morally entitled him to the presidency.

But Jackson's career marked so significant a turn in American history that we should first consider the growth of the western democracy which he represented.

FRESH WINDS FROM WESTERN FORESTS

One of the main events in the early years of the republic was the settlement of the region between the Appalachians and the Missouri Valley. Most of this area was still thickly wooded, though in parts of Illinois and increasingly in Iowa and eastern Kansas there were patches of grassy prairie. The settlement of the open plains to the Rockies, and of the Pacific coast, had to await a later generation. The center of population at the time of the first census was near Baltimore; by 1860 it was in Ohio, which was regarded a western state in Jackson's time, a central one in Lincoln's and an eastern one in McKinley's

One of the first steps was to get rid of the Indians. In part, their lands were bought; in part, they were seized by force. The woods themselves constituted a problem; they furnished timbers for the log cabins, but had to be cleared to permit farming. Sometimes this task was overdone; in parts of Michigan, for example, forest was cut down where the land was not suitable for agriculture. But most of the clearing was necessary. As one Ohio pioneer put the matter:

> None but those who have held the first plow, amid roots, stumps, stones and trees, while the faithful team was pulling and jerking it along . . . can really enjoy the delight that the same plowman feels while holding the plow as it moves along without a root or stump to obstruct it.

In the Southwest there were greater difficulties than in Ohio. Settlers often moved out as individuals, and so were more open to Indian attacks than where whole communities were settled. Kentucky was sometimes called the 'dark and bloody ground' because of the frequency of Indian wars.

In many parts of Europe the rural population lived in village communities and walked to the plowed fields. Not so in western America. There each homestead stood in the midst of its own lands, often miles away from the nearest neighbor. Rural isolation was one of the hardships of the pioneer. This was doubly hard on the women, who did not have the male privilege of hunting, fishing, and frequently riding to market. If pioneer life was selected by a particularly hardy type of men, this was even more true of the women. Since the men predominated, women acquired 'scarcity value' and were honored accordingly. Coeducation, equal property laws, women's suffrage, all began in the West.

By necessity, most houses were made by their owners, and most clothing was woven of homespun. For the housekeeping, let us cite another Ohio witness:

> We used to bake Indian pone, that is, bread made of rye and cornmeal . . . Our forks were two-tined. They weren't much good for holding some things. But, if we used our knives for conveying food to our mouths, it had to be done with the back of the knife to the face . . . Our starch was of two kinds – either made from flour or from grated potato . . . If one wants a light now, all one has to do is pull a string or press a button. Then, we had to pick up a coal with tongs, hold it against a candle, and blow. And one had to make the candles.

The influence of the West was in many ways salutary. For nearly a century the Northwest represented a society in which the common man had come into his own, and the only social distinction went to the pioneer who wielded the best axe or could shoot the straightest. But not all the influence of the West was good. There was much land grabbing and land gambling because of a restless spirit that forever sought greener pastures.

Above: It was a period of emigration to the West. In this fanciful scene, a well-fed, well-scrubbed family pauses on its journey to eat a meal of either game birds or deer. *Below:* In another idyllic view of pioneering homesteaders, the father has just brought home a deer for supper while others are clearing a forest in hopes of planting their crops. *Right:* Probably the first western American hero was Daniel Boone. In this scene he is shown protecting his family from a rampaging Indian. Boone once said that he had been 'ordained by God to settle

The pioneer's versatility led to a scorn of the expert. Charles Dickens and other European observers pointed out a marked deterioration in frontier manners.

What saved the West from degenerating into a land of hard-swearing, hard-drinking illiterates was the presence of the school and the church. To be sure, both were at first rather elementary. In the one-room log cabin school a young man, or perhaps a young woman, taught a dozen rowdy children with a spelling book and a birch rod, and the itinerant minister's whole library consisted of his Bible. But as each new settlement was planted, a public school was built as a matter of course, and the churches gave a touch of color to the drab lives of the pioneer women.

the wilderness,' and with 30 men had cut a road from the back country of North Carolina to the bluegrass region of Kentucky. *Below:* A frontier school room.

JACKSONIAN DEMOCRACY

John Quincy Adams was as honest and intelligent a man as ever went to the White House. He was the only president who may have become greater after his presidency – becoming the chief spokesman for the anti-slavery element in the House of Representatives. But he lacked the art of making himself popular, which Andrew Jackson possessed in abundance, so, after a single term, he went down before Jackson as his father had before Jefferson.

Andrew Jackson was typical of the West. He was born somewhere near the boundary between North and South Carolina but his entire active career was in his adopted state of Tennessee. He had dignity, courtesy and a fine reverence for women; but he fought duels, chased Indians into Florida and hanged deserters and British agents who aided the Indians. All previous presidents had been either from Virginia or Massachusetts, and men of education – if not wealthy, at least in easy

Opposite top: John Quincy Adams, the sixth president of the United States. *Left:* On his way to his inauguration in Washington DC, Andrew Jackson often stopped his coach to make impromptu speeches to village people. *Above:* Andrew Jackson, the seventh president of the United States.

circumstances. Jackson's victory at New Orleans in the War of 1812 had made him a national hero.

Elected president in 1824 he had an inauguration the following March that was a riotous scene of popular rejoicing. Conservative men were dismayed. Jefferson's opinions were bad enough, but the man himself was a scholar and a gentleman, even a philosopher. In no age or country is a scholar a 'common man.' He was for the people, but not of them. Everybody, however, could identify with Jackson. One sour eastern commentator, Philip Hone, said:

> President Jackson is certainly the most popular man we
> have ever known. Washington was not so much so . . .
> Here is a man who suits them exactly. He has a kind
> expression for each – the same for all, no doubt, but each
> thinks it intended for himself . . . Talk of him as the
> second Washington! It won't do now, Washington was
> only the first Jackson.

For all his immense popularity, Jackson had too impetuous a temper not to make enemies. A technical irregularity in his marriage to a divorced woman had caused political foes to brand him as an adulterer. When supercilious politicians snubbed Peggy Eaton, the former tavern girl who was the wife of one of the members of his cabinet, he championed her cause. Although he disliked Henry Clay and disapproved of his high tariff, when John C Calhoun of South Carolina threatened to nullify the tariff as unconstitutional, Jackson felt that his own authority had been flouted and declared, 'The federal Union, it must be preserved!' Calhoun left the vice presidency and Jackson replaced him with Martin Van Buren of New York, his eventual successor in the presidency.

Jackson also disapproved of a national bank, and he was the first president to make extensive removals from office on partisan grounds. Senator Marcy declared, 'to the victor belong the spoils of the vanquished,' and the whole system of partisan appointments became known as 'the spoils system.'

The opposition to Jackson crystallized into the new Whig Party, which took its name from the liberals of England. It had the faults of most opposition parties – a lack of unity on any one basis and the additional fault of repeatedly running military men with no political record for president. But it contained two giants, although neither quite reached the coveted presidency: Daniel Webster of Massachusetts, the greatest of American orators, and Henry Clay of Kentucky, a deft politician and ingenious compromiser.

Great as was Jackson's personal influence, he was more the leader of the new democracy than its creator. Without him, some other western man, Clay perhaps, would have come to the presidency. The new movement showed its strength in various ways. One was universal men's suffrage, without the former property qualifications. Another was the multiplication of elective offices on the state and local level. This did not affect the federal government – voters had only the choice of presidential electors and of congressmen, since senators were still chosen by the state legislature. But state governors found that their assistants were chosen, not by themselves, but by the voters, and many town and county officers were also elected.

This worked fairly well in a rural America, where everyone knew his neighbors and could make a fair guess as to who would be the best sheriff, judge, school superintendent and road commissioner, but when America became citified it presented the voter with a long ballot of unfamiliar names, and in desperation he might vote the straight party ticket.

Finally, and not least important, was the new system of party nomination. The Congressional party caucus had ceased to function and a substitute was found in a party convention of members of the same party, chosen either directly or indirectly. Since Jackson's time, all parties, great and small, have nominated candidates for president and vice president in party conventions. The result has been to choose less regularly from the cabinet and Congress, and more commonly to pick state governors or eminent generals.

The Whigs resembled the old Federalists in championing a national bank, a high protective tariff and internal improvements at federal expense. But they differed in one respect. The Federalists had been avowedly aristocratic; The Whigs courted popular favor by methods quite as demagogic as those of the Democrats.

This was exemplified in the campaign of 1840. The Whigs nominated William Henry Harrison of Ohio, a former Indian fighter who had won the battle of Tippecanoe. Answering a Democratic taunt, the Whigs boasted that Harrison was a simple pioneer who lived in a log cabin and drank hard cider. Actually he was the descendant of Virginia gentlemen, the owner of a good frame house, a man of scholarly and somewhat pedantic speech. For vice president they chose John Tyler, an anti-Jackson, states rights Democrat, and rode to victory on the cry 'Tippecanoe and Tyler too!' But elderly General Harrison died almost immediately and the Whigs were saddled with 'Tyler too' for almost the whole term. When Tyler came out against the national bank, the cabinet resigned – with the exception of Webster, the Secretary of State, who wanted to complete negotiations with Great Britain on the Maine boundary. This was the Webster-Ashburton Treaty.

Opposite top: John Tyler, the tenth president of the United States. *Opposite left below:* William Henry Harrison was the ninth president. Although his political views were neither extreme nor deeply held, one would not have known that by looking at this poster advertising a meeting in Alton, Illinois. Note also the inference that he had grown up in a log cabin. *Below:* Harrison rose to fame as a general in the War of 1812 after which he was both a Congressman and Senator from Ohio. *Right:* The *Hard Cider and Log Cabin Almanac for 1841.* It had been said that Harrison was a 'log-cabin, hard-cider candidate.'

THE ROAD TO OREGON

In 1844 the Democrats returned to their accustomed glory and elected James Polk of Tennessee as an advocate of expansion. Almost any people but the restless Americans would long have been content with the Louisiana Purchase from France in 1803 and the purchase of Florida from Spain in 1819. But pioneers were already dreaming of the warm, wet Pacific coast – the Oregon Territory belonging to British America, and California and the Southwest controlled by Mexico.

The region between Mexican California and Russian Alaska had not been precisely divided. Both British and Americans had explored the area, traded with Indian tribes and made some settlements such as the missionary station of Marcus Whitman. The British were represented chiefly by the Hudson's Bay Company, trading for furs.

American claims extended over the whole Oregon Territory, and a popular expansionist slogan was 'Fifty-four forty or fight!' this being the southern limit of Russian Alaska. But Polk and his government had no serious intention of entering into a doubtful war with so powerful a nation as Britain. A common sense compromise was effected, extending the northern frontier of the United States along the 49th parallel of latitude clear to the Pacific coast, leaving Vancouver Island to the British.

Settlement followed rapidly. The emigrants had no intention of stopping on the treeless Great Plains, still less so in the forbidding Rockies. They wanted good land to plow, mild weather and abundant woodlands. So they undertook a long trek, starting at some such point as Omaha on

the Missouri with the earliest grass of spring. They went in canvas-covered wagons, carrying household goods, flour and seed for the first planting.

Their wagons were usually drawn by oxen – slow beasts, but tough and strong. Whole companies often traveled together for protection from the Indians. They expected to reach Independence Rock in Wyoming by the Fourth of July so that they would have a good prospect of establishing their new homes by winter. Their greatest peril was fording the swift and treacherous Snake River, a branch of the Oregon or Columbia, where men were often drowned.

The American portion of the Northwest was divided into the territories, later the states, of Oregon, Washington and Idaho; the British portion formed the present Canadian province of British Columbia. Because of their northerly location, these territories were closed to slavery.

Not so the lands acquired from Mexico. But before taking up the annexation of Texas and the subsequent Mexican War, let us look at the type of politics and society which was developing in the South.

Left: By the 1830s the Oregon Trail was in heavy use. A view of a wagon train at the Devil's Gate landmark by the Sweetwater River a few miles west of Independence Rock in central Wyoming. *Opposite below:* A cartoon, *Ultimatum on the Oregon Question*, printed in 1846.

Below: Fresh meat seemed to be abundant on the Oregon Trail, as this drawing of buffalo hunters testifies.

KING COTTON AND HIS DOMAIN

In the days of Jefferson and Madison, many regarded the primary division of the country as that of East and West. But this proved of far less importance than that between North and South. There were two reasons for this. The West had no special and endangered economic interest such as the South had with its slavery. Also the West was a 'dissolving view'; constant migration had pushed it farther and farther away from the Appalachians. But the division between North and South was relatively constant; individuals often moved from one section to another, but there

Below: Cotton was king in the state of Mississippi. *Opposite:* El Whitney, the inventor of the cotton gin, in 1821 at the age of 55. Prior to his invention of the gin in 1793, the main crops in the South had been tobacco, rice and indigo. But now cotton came into its own.

80

was no mass movement in either direction.

In the East the line of division was Mason and Dixon's survey line between Maryland and Pennsylvania, then along the Ohio River, then along the northern border of Missouri and thence westward on the parallel of 36° 30'' to the Rockies. North of this line slavery had disappeared.

When we think of the South we picture some great cotton plantation worked by hundreds of slaves. But this was only part of the South. Maryland, Virginia and North Carolina continued to specialize in tobacco, Kentucky in horses, Missouri in mules and western Texas in cattle. Where the soil was poor there were many little hardscrabble farms, worked by their owners or, at most, the labor of a few slave families. 'King Cotton' began in South Carolina, spread through the richer lands in Georgia,

Left: Slaves were put to work using the cotton gin. *Below:* Still other slaves were sent out into the fields to pick the cotton. *Center bottom:* The cartoon shows a slave auction in South Carolina. At the right are the

Alabama, Mississippi, Louisiana and southeastern Texas.

When the Yankee Eli Whitney invented his cotton cleaning cotton gin he had, unwittingly, strengthened slavery. For now, this became the richest staple crop. Owners of cotton plantations formed a new aristocracy of wealth and lived in relatively luxurious homes with imported silver and glassware, family portraits and excellent furniture. The owner lived an open-air life; he loved to ride, hunt and shoot. Nearly all the populous cities were in the North. The plantation, like the medieval manor, was almost self-sustaining. There were slave carpenters, horse doctors, gardeners, cooks and tailors. In the phrase of Professor Ulrich Philips, the South 'was rural, but not rustic.'

The owner of a plantation was seldom idle. It took time to look after and manage the slaves and the plantation business; besides, like his British equivalent, the country squire, he took an active interest in local and national politics. The religious skepticism of Jefferson's day disappeared; now the South was almost solidly evangelical Protestant, and suspicious of New England Unitarianism. It produced more than its numerical quota of army officers, active politicians and orators – perhaps less than its quota of scholars, authors and intellectuals.

On some large plantations the detailed management of the slaves was left to hired overseers; and the trading in slaves fell into the hands of a class of slave dealers, socially scorned even by the owners who dealt with them. How well or badly were the slaves treated? No general answer can be given, because each plantation was a law unto itself. The laws were frankly repressive. A patrol was kept up to prevent slaves from going abroad at night without their master's permission; in some states it was forbidden to teach slaves to read – freedmen might easily fall again into slavery. And, although the laws forbade excessive cruelty to slaves, no slave's testimony was received in court, so such cases could not easily be prosecuted.

parents of the young man on the block. At the rear, flapping in the breeze, is a flag bearing the wry comment 'All men are free and equal.' *Below right*: A poster announcing a slave auction in New Oreleans.

In general, it may be said that the actual conduct of many plantation owners was more merciful than the laws – many owners taught their slaves to read and write and some planters boasted that none were sold away from the plantations where they were born.

Since the majority of white southerners owned no slaves, it may be asked why they followed the lead of the plantation owners in politics. The answer seems to be that slavery appealed to many in the South as a necessary police measure to prevent a racial uprising. They often referred to French Haiti, where the disappearance of slavery was followed by the creation of a black state and the subversion of the white man's civilization. In certain mountainous districts such as western Virginia, eastern Kentucky and eastern Tennessee, where slaves were few, there was small attachment to the institution. But even the 'poor white' in the Deep South feared the economic competition and the lack of political discipline of the black freedman.

So, for the most part, wealthy plantation owner, independent yeoman, impoverished 'cracker' and restless pioneer felt a certain unity as children of the South, and this was the most determining factor in American history for the generation preceding the Civil War.

BY HEWLETT & BRIGHT.

SALE OF VALUABLE SLAVES,

(On account of departure)

The Owner of the following named and valuable Slaves, being on the eve of departure for Europe, will cause the same to be offered for sale, at the NEW EXCHANGE, corner of St. Louis and Chartres streets, on *Saturday*, May 16, at Twelve o'Clock, *viz.*

1. SARAH, a mulatress, aged 45 years, a good cook and accustomed to house work in general, is an excellent and faithful nurse for sick persons, and in every respect a first rate character.

2. DENNIS, her son, a mulatto, aged 24 years, a first rate cook and steward for a vessel, having been in that capacity for many years on board one of the Mobile packets; is strictly honest, temperate, and a first rate subject.

3. CHOLE, a mulatress, aged 36 years, she is, without exception, one of the most competent servants in the country, a first rate washer and ironer, does up lace, a good cook, and for a bachelor who wishes a house-keeper she would be invaluable: she is also a good ladies' maid, having travelled to the North in that capacity.

4. FANNY, her daughter, a mulatress, aged 16 years, speaks French and English, is a superior hair-dresser, (pupil of Guilliac,) a good seamstress and ladies' maid, is smart, intelligent, and a first rate character.

5. DANDRIDGE, a mulatoo, aged 26 years, a first rate dining-room servant, a good painter and rough carpenter, and has but few equals for honesty and sobriety.

6. NANCY, his wife, aged about 24 years, a confidential house servant, good seamstress, mantuamaker and tailoress, a good cook, washer and ironer, etc.

7. MARY ANN, her child, a creole, aged 7 years, speaks French and English, is smart, active and intelligent.

8. FANNY or FRANCES, a mulatress, aged 22 years, is a first rate washer and ironer, good cook and house servant, and has an excellent character.

9. EMMA, an orphan, aged 10 or 11 years, speaks French and English, has been in the country 7 years, has been accustomed to waiting on table, sewing etc.: is intelligent and active.

10. FRANK. a mulatto, aged about 32 years speaks French and English, is a first rate hostler and coachman, understands perfectly well the management of horses, and is, in every respect, a first rate character, with the exception that he will occasionally drink, though not an habitual drunkard.

All the above named Slaves are acclimated and excellent subjects; they were purchased by their present vendor many years ago, and will, therefore, be severally warranted against all vices and maladies prescribed by law, save and except FRANK, who is fully guaranteed in every other respect but the one above mentioned.

TERMS:—One-half Cash, and the other half in notes at Six months, drawn and endorsed to the satisfaction of the Vendor, with special mortgage on the Slaves until final payment. The Acts of Sale to be passed before WILLIAM BOSWELL, *Notary Public*, at the expense of the Purchaser.

New-Orleans, May 13, 1835.

PRINTED BY BENJAMIN LEVY.

THE ROAD TO TEXAS

When Mexico seceded from Spain it carried two liabilities. Its north-eastern boundary was ill-defined, and it took several generations to establish a stable government. Many Americans settled in the vast region known as Texas, a transition zone between the cotton kingdom of the South and the cattle-raising West. Mexico claimed their allegiance, but the constant disorder of Mexican politics made them determined to set up their own government.

This led to war. The most picturesque incident was the siege of the Alamo, a fortified mission in San Antonio, where a small force of Texans fought to the last bullet against a much larger force of Mexican troops. For almost two weeks the beleaguered garrison held out, inflicting heavy casualties on General Santa Ana's troops, but at last they were over-whelmed and killed to the last man. Among the dead were the famous pioneer David Crockett; Colonel James Bowie, inventor of the Bowie knife; and Colonel Travis.

The war cry 'Remember the Alamo!' resounded through Texas. Samuel Houston avenged the slaughter at the battle of San Jacinto. This victory assured Texan independence, and for several years (1836–45) Texas was an independent republic, with a flag bearing a single star.

President Houston was a singular and most interesting man. Although he had fought in Indian wars, he was a friend to the Indians and an adopted son of the Cherokee. He had been governor of Tennessee, but resigned because of his wife's desertion. After the annexation of Texas by the United States he remained governor, but was deposed for resisting the seccessionist movement in 1861. Houston, Texas, the largest city of the Southwest, bears his name.

The annexation of Texas to the United States was inevitable. It was also inevitable that it would be a slave state, since most of its settlers came from the South. This fact caused some misgivings among anti-slavery nor-therners; but the majority of Texans were keen for it. Texas was admitted without having to pass through the territorial stage, and permitted to keep her public lands under state control.

Below: Most of the Americans who had emigrated to Texas found that Mexican rule was oppressive. They declared the independence of Texas from Mexico, 2 March 1836. By this time war had already begun and Santa Ana was besieging the Alamo at San Antonio. The Alamo was an abandoned mission that had been fortified against attack. There, for nearly two weeks, 188 Texans held off 3000 Mexicans. In the end, every member of the defending garrison was massacred. *Opposite:* Col James Bowie, the frontier scout and inventor of the Bowie knife, who was one of the American fighters killed at the Battle of the Alamo.

Overleaf: Santa Ana standing before Sam Houston. At San Jacinto, 21 April 1836, a Texas army of less than 800 men, under Gen Houston, raising the battle cry 'Remember the Alamo!' defeated a force of 1200 Mexicans and captured Santa Ana.

THE MEXICAN WAR

The annexation of Texas in 1845 did not satisfy the Americans. They were already looking toward California, still in Mexican possession. Polk's administration offered to buy the whole Southwest, but Mexican pride, wounded by the Texas affair, caused them to refuse. A boundary dispute between Texas and Mexico led to some fighting; Polk thereupon declared that 'American blood has been shed on American soil,' which rather begged the question: Was it American soil?

The war which followed (1846–48) was brief and one-sided. Although the United States had vastly superior numbers and resources, had the Mexicans been united they might have prolonged the struggle, owing to the rugged and mountainous character of the country.

Two generals, Winfield Scott, nicknamed 'Old Fuss and Feathers' from his concern for military forms, and Zachary Taylor, nicknamed 'Old Rough and Ready' from his neglect of such forms, carried the American forces to victory. Unfortunately for the Polk administration, both generals were Whigs, and Taylor was elected president in 1848. It is interesting to note that many of the officers on both sides of the Civil War had received their baptism of fire in the Mexican conflict. Robert E Lee and Ulysses S Grant both served, and John Frémont effected a diversion in California.

By the Treaty of 1848 the United States annexed the area now consisting of California, New Mexico, Arizona, Nevada, Utah and small parts of Colorado and Wyoming. In partial compensation, Mexico was awarded 15 million dollars. A few years later there was a small additional purchase to facilitate a southern railroad route. This 'Gadsden Purchase' com-

Left: Zachary Taylor, the twelfth president of the United States. *Above:* The United States Army on the march to the Mexican War. War had been declared when President Polk put the blame on Mexico for the fighting that had broken out between Mexicans and Gen Taylor's troops along the border in May 1846. The war lasted until the signing of the treaty of Guadaloupe Hidalgo 2 February 1848, in which Mexico agreed that the border between the two countries would be the Rio Grande, and ceded New Mexico and California, as well as the land that lay between them to the United States. In turn, the United States government paid the Mexican government $15 million.

pleted the territory of the continental United States; subsequent annex-
ations were separated from the rest of the country by sea (Hawaii) or by
Canada (Alaska).

The story of the Mormons in Utah is a unique chapter in American
history. Joseph Smith professed to find in *The Book of Mormon* a new
revelation. His followers were driven out of the eastern and middle
western states, partly because of their religious tenets, but mainly because
they allowed the practice of poligamy. In 1847 Brigham Young led them to
the region of the Great Salt Lake in what is now Utah, but was then called
'Deseret'. Here the Latter Day Saints, as they called themselves, or
Mormons, as the rest of the world called them, established a wilderness
Zion, strictly and almost autocratically disciplined. It became a thriving
agricultural community and, for a time, kept out the non-Mormons, or
'gentiles.'

Left: Gen Winfield Scott at Vera Cruz, Mexico. President Polk had decided to open a second front in Mexico, in addition to the one along the Texas border. He sent Scott and his expeditionary force from New Orleans to Vera Cruz. With his army of 10,000 men, Scott headed west from Vera Cruz toward Mexico City. When he reached Cerro Gordo, Santa Ana attacked on 17–18 April 1847 and was soundly defeated. Scott then took Jalapa and Puebla. When Scott and his troops reached Mexico City, Santa Ana attacked again and was defeated again. Scott then won a succession of victories:

Contreras (19 August),
Churubusco (20 August),
Molino del Rey
(8 September) and
Chapultepec (13
September). On 14
September 1847 the
Americans had captured
the Mexican capital city.
Above: Gen Zachary
Taylor had been invading
Mexico from the north.
'Old Rough and Ready'
captured Matamoros, and
then with a handful of
regulars and several
thousand volunteers he
began his siege of
Monterey. After three
days of hard fighting,
21–23 September, he
captured the city. *Right:*
Gen Winfield Scott
entering Mexico City in
triumph.

Left: Brigham Young, Mormon prophet Joseph Smith's second in command, decided that it would be best if the Mormons left Illinois and headed west. *Above:* This they did in 1846. About 15,000 of them left their homes, crossed through Iowa to the Council Bluffs area. *Opposite top:* In 1847 Young and a small group of his followers pushed west across the plains, over the mountains, and finally reached the Great Salt Lake. Two larger groups followed them, reaching the lake by autumn. *Opposite bottom:* There they built their city – Salt Lake City. By 1850 more than 11,000 Mormons were living in the Great Salt Lake Valley. By the time that the transcontinental railroad was completed in 1869, there were 60,000 Mormons there.

THE DISPUTE OVER TERRITORIES

In acquiring Texas, California and the territories between, the nation also acquired a new political dispute. Should these vast regions be open or closed to slavery? The point of view of anti-slavery northerners was pretty well expressed in James Russell Lowell's *Biglow Papers*:

> They just want this Californy
>   So's to lug new slave states in,
> To abuse ye, and to scorn ye,
>   And to plunder ye like sin!

It was long held in the North that President Polk's war was an attempt on the part of southern politicians, and mainly southern volunteers, to widen the area of southern influence. The actual situation was a little more complex. Most Americans, regardless of section, favored any American expansion, and a few southerners, such as Senator John C Calhoun of South Carolina, dreaded that acquiring new territory in the southwest

Left: John C Calhoun, the
powerful senator from
South Carolina, later vice-
president under both
John Quincy Adams and
Andrew Jackson. *Opposite
bottom:* San Francisco was
a bustling little town in
1851 just after Henry
Clay's 'Compromise of
1850' in which California
was admitted as a free
state 9 September 1850.
Right: The newly-elected
James K Polk, the eleventh
president of the United
States, watches benignly
as expansionists threaten
Oregon, and as John
C Calhoun, the then
Secretary of State, rides
out of the Cabinet.

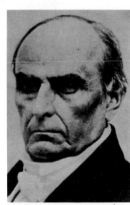

Top: Daniel Webster.
Above: Henry Clay.
Webster, the great orator,
was first a representative
in Congress from New
Hampshire and later both
a congressman and senator
from Massachusetts. Clay
was a powerful senator
from Kentucky.

might reopen the slavery dispute and feed the fires of abolitionism.

In any event, this is what happened. David Wilmot of Pennsylvania introduced a resolution favoring freedom for California and all the other territories acquired from Mexico (Texas was already a slave state). This precipitated a bitter controversy and there was talk of a southern secession if the 'Wilmot Proviso' were enacted.

Three veteran politicians rushed into the breach to patch up a compromise similar to the Missouri Compromise of 1820, which had kept the slave question within bounds for a generation. Daniel Webster, Henry Clay and John C Calhoun offered solutions. In the meantime, President Taylor had died, and the question came up in the time of Millard Fillmore, his vice-presidential successor.

Clay worked out the details of this 'Compromise of 1850.' California was to be admitted, as she wished, as a free state. The new territories were to be organized without reference to the slave question. The Texas boundaries were readjusted. The slave trade, though not slavery itself, was to be barred from the District of Columbia and federal marshals were empowered to capture fugitive slaves in the North, in case local officials failed to act.

All this was accepted, even the bitter dose of the fugitive slave law, by Daniel Webster for the North. But Calhoun desired more; either the North must cease to agitate for abolition or each section should have a veto on the acts of the other – an arrangement similar to the two consuls of the old Roman Republic. Webster's acquiescence caused bitter criticism from anti-slavery men. The poet John Greenleaf Whittier spoke of Webster as a fallen archangel; the attempt to recapture a fugitive slave in Massachusetts called out a large force of soldiers and Harriet Beecher Stowe wrote the most widely circulated American novel of the generation, *Uncle Tom's Cabin*, as a protest against the law.

A few politicians, North and South, accepted the compromise of 1850 as a 'final solution' of the slavery question, but the country at large was more shaken by it than ever before. The entire decade of the 1850s was full of sectional agitation, leading directly, and perhaps inevitably, to war in the 1860s.

THE SLAVERY QUESTION.

Pl.4.

DON QUIXOTTE:

„I bet Cuba!"

JOHN BULL:

„I bet Canada!"

Go it, my Boy, you will beat them all!

THE UNION FOR EVER!

Above: A political cartoon of 1844 entitled *Great Prize-Fight of the American Eagle Against the Wolf and the Alligator.* The question was which new states would be admitted to the union as slave states and which would not be. Spain (the alligator) and England (the wolf in sheep's clothing) are being accused of meddling in the resolution of the problem. *Left:* Slaves were often badly treated. The title of this engraving is *Barbarity Committed on a Free African, who was Found on the Ensuing Morning, by the Side of the Road, Dead! Opposite top:* The caricature appeared after the Dred Scott decision of 1857 and was entitled *Conquering Prejudice* or *Fulfilling a Constitutional Duty with*

Alacrity. It pictures two sanctimonious white men pursuing a slave and her baby. The slave says, 'My God! My Child! Will no one help! Is there no mercy!' The man in the middle remarks, 'Any man can perform an agreeable duty – it is not everyone that can perform a disagreeable duty.' The man at the right observes, 'By Heaven! He exceeds my most sanguine expectation. He marks his way so clearly and treads so loyally on the track of the Constitution. It is more than great – it is sublime. I feel a great sense of relief.' *Right:* A poster from 1851 warning black people of the powers of the Boston police. *Far right:* The frontispiece of *Pictures and Stories from Uncle Tom's Cabin.*

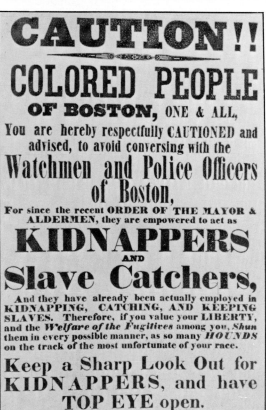

CAUTION!!
COLORED PEOPLE
OF BOSTON, ONE & ALL,

You are hereby respectfully CAUTIONED and advised, to avoid conversing with the

Watchmen and Police Officers of Boston,

For since the recent ORDER OF THE MAYOR & ALDERMEN, they are empowered to act as

KIDNAPPERS
AND
Slave Catchers,

And they have already been actually employed in KIDNAPPING, CATCHING, AND KEEPING SLAVES. Therefore, if you value your LIBERTY, and the *Welfare of the Fugitives* among you, *Shun* them in every possible manner, as so many *HOUNDS* on the track of the most unfortunate of your race.

Keep a Sharp Look Out for KIDNAPPERS, and have TOP EYE open.

APRIL 24, 1851.

UTOPIAS IN THE BACKWOODS

Slavery, where it existed, was a damper on reform agitations in general. Therefore, these were largely confined to the North. In the 1830s, 1840s and 1850s, a wide variety of philanthropic, humanitarian and even collectivist movements attracted support from working men and intellectuals.

Imprisonment for debt was outlawed in many states; education was made more general; reforms were made in the treatment of prisoners, paupers and insane persons. In 1848 there was the beginning of a women's suffrage movement, although it was many years before it became nation-wide. The so-called 'Maine Law' was a local experiment in the prohibition of intoxicating drinks.

Most striking was the establishment of small voluntary communities on a cooperative basis – such were Brooke Farm in Massachusetts and New Harmony in Indiana. These ran parallel to the propaganda of Comte Saint-Simon, François Fourier and Robert Owen in Europe, and are collectively known as 'Utopian Socialism'. Except for the collective ownership of property, it had little in common with the militant Socialism associated with Karl Marx. It made no appeal to class feeling, and did not call for any political action. Each group consisted of volunteers who withdrew from the capitalist and competitive world to organize work and life in common.

There were many movements toward the simplification of life associated with the philosophical school, born in Germany, labeled Transcendentalism, preached by the essayist, Ralph Waldo Emerson and the individualist writer Henry David Thoreau. Many adopted teetotalism, abstaining from all alcoholic beverages, and a few added vegetarianism. There was a tendency to take an interest in more or less heretical schools of medicine, such as homeopathy and osteopathy, and phrenology, a premature attempt to map the brain into separate areas, had its adherents.

In religion, the stern orthodox Calvinism of the early New England Puritans was, in some cases, softened into Universalism, denying Hell, and Unitarianism, denying the Trinity. But there was no great increase in materialism, in the European sense, for nearly all the reformers were idealistic.

Above left: New Harmony, Indiana was conceived by Robert Owen, the reforming British industrialist, as a social experiment in community living which he hoped might solve the labor-capital movement. It attracted intellectuals, tradesmen, and artisans, as well as numerous cranks and strange visionaries. *Above:* a lithograph made by Nathaniel Currier which he called *Shakers Near Lebanon*. The Shakers originated in England in 1758, founded by Mother Ann Lee. She and eight female followers came to America and set up a community whose tenets were celibacy, equality, neatness, simplicity and charity. Since celibacy was required, the only way of maintaining the Shaker population was through the recruitment of new members. *Right:* Henry David Thoreau was a New England writer who lived for a few months at Brook Farm, another experimental community. *Far right:* Ralph Waldo Emerson, the New England Transcendentalist, visited Brook Farm on numerous occasions.

THE BIRTH OF AMERICAN LITERATURE

Top left: Washington Irving was a journalist, author, satirist and man of society, known for his wit, humor and romanticism. He also was active in politics and diplomacy, serving as an attaché and later minister to Spain. *Left:* Edgar Allan Poe: poet, critic and short story writer. *Top right:* Nathaniel Hawthorne, one of the greatest American literary figures of the 19th century. He was most noted for his portrayal of New England Puritanism. *Above:* Ralph Waldo Emerson, the essayist and poet, was one of the founders of Transcendentalism. *Opposite top:* Walt Whitman, the master of free verse. *Opposite center:* James Fenimore Cooper, the author of historical romance and adventure. *Opposite bottom left:* Herman Melville, the author of *Moby Dick*. *Opposite far right:* A typical American whaler of his time.

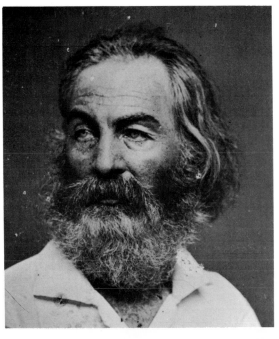

In the early 19th century, when American boastfulness was at its height, a liberal English clergyman, Sydney Smith, gave a word of caution. He asked, 'Who buys American manufactured goods and who reads an American book?' A generation later no one would have asked this scornful question, for, in the years before the Civil War, the United States produced literature of notable quality, read and admired on both sides of the Atlantic.

The beginnings of American literature centered in New England, and were closely connected with the reform movements discussed in the last chapter. Ralph Waldo Emerson, John Greenleaf Whittier and James Russell Lowell were abolitionists, and Henry David Thoreau actually went to jail for refusing to pay taxes to a government which sanctioned slavery.

Others were less directly connected with reform. Nathaniel Hawthorne explored the Puritan past with the dark lantern of imagination. His story, *The Scarlet Letter*, has been termed by some good critics the greatest American novel. Edgar Allan Poe, poet and writer of short stories, is mainly associated with Maryland; his tales were 'out of space, out of time.' He excelled in the weird, the macabre, and was virtually the inventor of the detective story.

Another excellent short story writer was Washington Irving, author of *Rip Van Winkle* and *The Legend of Sleepy Hollow*. With less artistry, but making freer use of American material, James Fenimore Cooper celebrated the frontiersman and the native Indian. Less noticed in their own time were Herman Melville, the author of *Moby Dick*, superficially a seafaring story but containing a symbolic study of man's search for the infinite; and Emily Dickinson, whose imaginative poetry was published mainly after her death.

Probably the most popular poets of the time were Henry Wadsworth Longfellow, the best of the narrative poets, who turned to American and Scandinavian antiquity for his themes (in his *Hiawatha* he combined both; the substance of Indian folklore and the form of the Finnish *Kalevala*); and William Cullen Bryant, the poet of nature.

Distinctly different from these was Walt Whitman, the first great American to use free verse, not only without rhyme, but with irregular rhythms. His *Leaves of Grass*, symbolizing American democracy, surprised, and at first offended, a public accustomed to more conventional poetry.

Americans made their mark in history, also. Eminent among these were Francis Parkman, who specialized in colonial French America; William Prescott, who did a similar service for Spanish colonization; and John Lothrop Motley, who chronicled *The Rise of the Dutch Republic*.

THE 'IRREPRESSIBLE CONFLICT'

Civil wars and revolutions, like foreign wars, are often preceded by a decade or so of extreme political tension, or 'cold war.' We have seen this to be true of the American Revolution in the years between the end of the French and Indian War (1763) and the actual outbreak of hostilities in 1775. Sectional strife, chiefly over slavery in the territories, filled the 1850s. This was termed by one eminent anti-slavery leader, William H Seward of New York, 'an irrepressible conflict,' and by another, Abraham Lincoln of Illinois, 'a house divided against itself.'

Nearly all political leaders still strove to hold the Union together. The three great senators of 1850 – Clay, Webster and Calhoun – had passed from the scene, but the three most prominent men of the 1850s were northern Democrats who were not enemies of slavery. Presidents Franklin Pierce of New Hampshire, elected in 1852, and James Buchanan of Pennsylvania, elected in1856, made many concessions to southern sentiment; so much so, that angry anti-slavery men called them 'doughfaces' for having no political expression' at all. Stephen A Douglas of Illinois, perhaps abler and certainly more popular than either, reached for the White House but never attained it.

Douglas, who said that he did not care whether 'slavery is voted up or down,' was interested in a northern route for a railroad to the Pacific. In order to attract southern support he urged the prairie territories of Kansas and Nebraska be organized without reference to slavery. They had been free under the Missouri Compromise of 1820, but their status should be determined by the vote of the white settlers. This he termed 'popular sovereignty;' his opponents called it 'squatter sovereignty,' a squatter being an unauthorized settler on public lands.

This Kansas-Nebraska measure started a rush for Kansas. Pro-slavery men, chiefly from the slave state of Missouri, poured in to vote for slavery;

Top left: Stephen A Douglas, the Democratic Senator from Illinois, had broken with President Buchanan over his policy in Kansas. The Republicans in the East were so pleased with Douglas' new policy that they urged their friends in Illinois not to oppose him for re-election. But the Illinois Republicans selected Abraham Lincoln to run against him in 1858. Lincoln then challenged Douglas to a series of debates. Accounts of these debates appeared in nearly every metropolitan paper in the country, and although Douglas was eventually the winner of the campaign, Lincoln acquitted himself so well that the debates served to build his fame throughout the country. *Top right:* One of the chief disagreements between Douglas and Lincoln was Douglas' espousal of the doctrine of Popular Sovereignty. *Above:* Franklin Pierce, the fourteenth president of the United States. *Opposite top: Tyrants Prostrate, Liberty Triumphant,* a cartoon of 1844. Popular forces in the state of Rhode Island had staged a demonstration known as Dorr's Rebellion in 1843. *Opposite bottom:* Many people believe that the birth of the Repulican Party happened at an 'Anti-Nebraska' mass meeting in this building in Ripon, Wisconsin, 28 February 1854.

anti-slavery easterners came to make Kansas free. Nebraska, by its geographical location, was assumed to be free; but Kansas literally became a battleground. Here there was a miniature civil war, a sort of curtain raiser to the great Civil War. Slavery men burned the free settlement of Lawrence and shot some of its settlers; in retaliation the fanatic John Brown murdered slave state immigrants, some of whom were not even slave owners themselves.

Senator Charles Sumner of Massachusetts made a fiery speech on the 'crime against Kansas,' and was hammered into unconsciousness by a cane in the hands of Preston Brooks of South Carolina. Douglas demanded a free and honest vote on the part of Kansas, and thus became hostile to President Pierce, who was determined to concede the territory to the South.

A main result of the Kansas question was the organization of a new political party. The old Whig Party was now hopelessly split between its northern and southern wings. An attempt to create a new American Party, hostile to foreign immigration, and especially to the Irish Roman Catholics had some success, but soon faded. All the anti-slavery forces united in 1854 to form a new party, which revived the original name of Jefferson's Republican Party. Initial meetings were held in the Middle West at Jackson, Michigan and Ripon, Wisconsin. Its platform was essentially that of the little third party, the Free Soilers, to keep the territories free

Left: Col Charles Sumner, the Senator from Massachusetts, on a visit to Kansas. Sumner had made a four-hour address to the Senate urging the repeal of the Fugitive Slave Law on 19–20 May 1856. In the speech he talked of the 'Crime Against Kansas,' and denounced Senator Andrew P Butler of South Carolina charging 'shameful imbecility.' His remarks enraged Congressman Preston Brooks, a relative of Butler. He approached Sumner in the Senate Chamber, criticized him for slander and beat him over the head with a cane. Sumner fell to the floor covered with blood and his injuries were so serious that he could not resume his duties for five years. *Opposite below:* Senator Charles Sumner. *Below:* James Buchanan, the fifteenth president of the United States. *Below right:* John C Frémont, the Republican candidate for president in 1856, was the one who surveyed the Oregon Trail in 1842 and became known as 'The Pathfinder of the West.' In 1856 he led a party of explorers into California, which was then under Mexican rule. When war between Mexico and the United States had been declared, he was appointed military governor of California, but was court-martialed for insubordination and resigned his commission.

from slavery; but it was joined by the great bulk of northern Whigs, like Seward and Lincoln, and by many anti-slavery northern Democrats.

Their candidate in 1856 was John Charles Frémont, a southerner by birth, but associated with the far West. He had mapped routes for exploration across the Rocky Mountains and was nicknamed 'The Pathfinder'. He was defeated by James Buchanan, who carried the South and some key states in the North. Frémont won New England, New York, and many other free states. Whittier was jubilant: 'If months have well nigh won the field, what may not four years do?'

Since in this generation we are accustomed to think of Republicans as a conservative party associated with business interests, it is interesting to note that the Republicans of the 1850s were called 'The Radicals,' especially in the South, and cartooned as a motley array of socialists, abolitionists, feminists and other extremists. The richer capitalists were, in fact, almost the last northerners to join the party because they feared an anti-slavery triumph might lead to the secession of the South and the breakup of the Union.

A great deal of American history is told by legal cases before the Supreme Court. One of the most important of these was the Dred Scott Decision, arranged by both sides in order to bring to an issue the status of slavery in the territories. Dred Scott, a slave, had been brought into free territory and sued for his freedom on that account. The majority of the court, led by Chief Justice Taney, said that a black man had not the privilege of suing in a federal court, and further, that since slaves were 'property,' no territory could bar them; only a state would have such authority.

A PUBLIC MEETING

WILL BE HELD ON

THURSDAY EVENING, 2D INSTANT,

at 7 o'clock, in ISRAEL CHURCH, to consider the atrocious decision of the Supreme Court in the

DRED SCOTT CASE,

and other outrages to which the colored people are subject under the Constitution of the United States.

C. L. REMOND,
ROBERT PURVIS,

and others will be speakers on the occasion. Mrs. MOTT, Mr. M'KIM and B. S. JONES of Ohio. have also accepted invitations to be present.

All persons are invited to attend. Admittance free.

Left: Feeling ran high after the Supreme Court's decision in the Dred Scott case. *Above:* Chief Justice Roger Brooke Taney of the Supreme Court, the man who handed down the decision in the Dred Scott case. *Below:* Dred Scott and his wife. *Opposite:* A painting, *The Last Moments of John Brown,* by Thomas Hovenden.

This at once struck down the Missouri Compromise, which had established freedom in northern territories; the Republican plan of barring slavery by act of Congress from all territories; and Douglas's plan of local option on slavery. It made the extreme southern position law.

In a series of debates when they were running for senator from Illinois, Lincoln asked Douglas how his 'popular sovereignty' stood in the light of this decision. Douglas affected to make light of the question, saying that it did not matter how the Supreme Court might declare an abstract right for slavery, since the institution could not subsist unless supported by local laws to enforce it. This may have won Douglas a senate seat, but it probably lost him the presidency, for the South was now committed to the principle of universal slavery in the territories.

John Brown, who had led the free state 'Jayhawkers' to war in Kansas, now attempted a desperate enterprise in the East. He seized a federal arsenal at Harper's Ferry, Virginia. He had a plan to free and arm such slaves as could be reached. Of course, this petty rebellion was soon quashed and John Brown duly hanged. But it stirred a disproportionate excitement in both the North and the South. Some extreme northern abolitionists hailed Brown as a martyr; some southerners shuddered with memories of Nat Turner's rebellion, in which a number of white men had been killed in a slave insurrection.

Other national ties were snapping. Not only were old political parties rearranged, but also religious denominations. The two largest Protestant sects, the Methodists and the Baptists, organized separately along sectional lines.

Some southerners talked about restoring the balance of the sections by annexing Cuba from Spain or taking over some republic in Central America, which would then be open to slavery and the plantation system. Extremists even talked of reopening the slave trade, although this was still opposed by the southern majority. On the other hand, some northerners organized an 'underground railway' to help slaves escape to Canada, and favored 'personal liberty laws' which denied the aid of local officers and jails in case federal forces recaptured fugitive slaves.

Below: Stephen A Douglas, the senator from Illinois and Democratic nominee for president in 1860. *Bottom:* An advertisement for the 'Underground Railroad' for smuggling slaves north to freedom in the 1850s. Despite its name, the Underground Railroad system did not usually rely on railroad trains. *Opposite top:* Most slaves walked north, as shown in the painting *The Underground Railroad. Opposite bottom:* Some escaping slaves were transported by boat. Slaves arriving at Camden, New Jersey on a ferry.

LIBERTY LINE.
NEW ARRANGEMENT---NIGHT AND DAY.

The improved and splendid Locomotives, Clarkson and Lundy, with their trains fitted up in the best style of accommodation for passengers, will run their regular trips during the present season, between the borders of the Patriarchal Dominion and Libertyville, Upper Canada. Gentlemen and Ladies, who may wish to improve their health or circumstances, by a northern tour, are respectfully invited to give us their patronage.

SEATS FREE, *irrespective of color.*

Necessary Clothing furnished gratuitously to such as have "*fallen among thieves.*"

"Hide the outcasts—let the oppressed go free."—*Bible.*

☞For seats apply at any of the trap doors, or to the conductor of the train.

J. CROSS, *Proprietor.*

N. B. For the special benefit of Pro-Slavery Police Officers, an extra heavy wagon for Texas, will be furnished, whenever it may be necessary, in which they will be forwarded as dead freight, to the "Valley of Rascals," always at the risk of the owners.

☞Extra Overcoats provided for such of them as are afflicted with protracted *chilly-phobia.*

THE REPUBLICAN TRIUMPH

In 1860 the Democratic Party which had dominated politics for 60 years suffered a division. A convention was held at Charleston, South Carolina – the very center of pro-slavery sentiment. Douglas was the leading candidate for the presidential nomination, but his insistence that slavery could, in fact if not in form, be nullified by the failure of a territory to enact a slave code, was an anathema to the South. After 57 futile ballots the party split; the Northern Democrats nominated Douglas, the Southern Democrats the vice president John Breckenridge of Kentucky.

This gave the Republicans their chance. William Henry Seward was the front runner, but in his political career he had made many enemies. Other aspirants were considered too radical or too conservative. An obvious compromise candidate was Lincoln: popular, a good speaker, moderate in opinion and from the key state of Illinois. As a British writer succinctly summed up the situation: 'The politicians did their usual deal and stumbled on the noble, tremendous *accident* of Abraham Lincoln!' Hannibal Hamlin of Maine was nominated for the vice presidency.

Below: President Buchanan did not want Stephen A Douglas to be nominated for president on the Democratic ticket, but Douglas was triumphant, and the 'Illinois Bantam' conquered the 'Old Cock' of the White House. Lincoln, at the right, is standing in the wings. *Opposite top:* A montage of the members of the thirty-sixth Senate of 1860. *Opposite bottom:* An etching: *The Last Hours of Congress, March, 1859.*

There was also a fourth party in the field. The Constitutional Union Party, frightened by the specter of national disruption, offered no platform at all, except 'the Union and the Constitution.' The voter thus had four choices: territorial freedom with the Republicans; local option on slavery with the Douglas Democrats; slavery in all territories with Breckenridge; or ignore the whole issue with Bell of Tennessee. It was probably the most important election in American history.

Lincoln was elected by a clear majority in the electoral college and he had a plurality, but no overall majority, of the popular vote. Douglas, the runner-up on the popular vote, carried only Missouri and part of New Jersey. Bell won some border slave states. Breckenridge carried the bulk of the South – Lincoln nearly all the North.

The Republicans had strengthened their position by adding to the anti-slavery cry, a homestead policy in the territories by which a settler could, after a certain number of years, gain a freehold on government land without having to pay for it. They also approved a protective tariff, which probably ensured them Pennsylvania.

In those days there were about four months between an election and the inauguration. Buchanan, though his party had been defeated at the polls, still held office. How, in this interim would the South react? Would it accept the verdict of the polls, or secede? And what would the president do in the latter case? Now let us look at this new man from the West, of whom the nation at large still knew so little.

ABRAHAM LINCOLN: THE NEW MAN FROM THE WEST

Abraham Lincoln was born in Kentucky in 1809. He was not the only American president to rise from humble beginnings; in fact, ever since Jackson's time, this has been more the rule than the exception. But, at first, Lincoln did not seem to have much prospect of success. His father was a typical wandering pioneer, never long settled in any place. Abraham's home was a log cabin, his schooling almost nonexistant. From Kentucky the family moved to Indiana and then to Illinois. Lincoln read incessantly, studied law, and became a popular local lawyer, nicknamed 'Honest Abe,' and 'The Railsplitter.'

He was elected to one term in Congress, the highest office he filled before the presidency. He vied for a senatorship with Stephen A Douglas, who defeated him (in those days senators were still chosen by the state legislatures), but their debates attracted national attention. Up to this point, he could well be described in the words of the poet Stephen Vincent Benét:

> The small town lawyer, the crude small town politician.
> State character but comparative failure at forty
> In spite of ambition enough for twenty Caesars,
> Honesty rare as a man without self-pity,
> Kindness as large and plain as a prairie wind,
> And a self-confidence like an iron bar.

Lincoln was an anti-slavery man, but no abolitionist. He thought that there was no constitutional power to forbid slavery in the states, but he wanted to keep it out of all the territories and hoped that it might 'wither on the vine' in the few older states which still held to it.

Personally, Lincoln was a paradox. A tall, lean, lanky man, apparently awkward and unsystematic, inexperienced in high public offices, ill at ease in his 'store clothes,' he had the keenest insight into the popular mind of any man of his time. Famous as a jester and teller of good stories, his most marked personal trait was a constitutional melancholy, almost suicidal in his early days.

Lincoln had to wait in the wings, unable to act, for the four months before his inauguration. In the meantime President Buchanan did nothing. It must be admitted that Buchanan's position was difficult; he would either have to permit the secession of such states as chose to break away from the Union, or present the new administration with a war. His party had been defeated and he was, as the phrase goes, a 'lame duck' president.

When he took office, Lincoln did two things. He appointed a strong cabinet of national leaders, and was not afraid to include some of his own rivals for the nomination. He made a conciliatory inaugural address, inviting the seceding states to have a second thought and return.

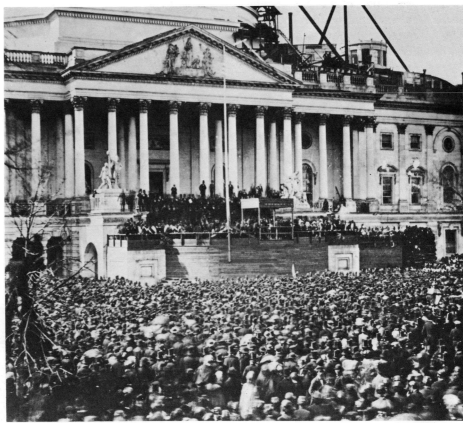

Opposite top left: Lincoln's birthplace was a log cabin near Hodgenville, Kentucky. The cabin at the Lincoln Birthplace Historic Site is a replica of the one in which he was born. Soon after he was nominated for the presidency, he wrote an autobiography which began: 'Abraham Lincoln was born 12 February 1809, then in Hardin, now in the more recently formed county of Larue, Kentucky. His father, Thomas, & grandfather Abraham, were born in Rockingham county, Virginia, whither their ancestors had come from Bucks County Pennsylvania. His lineage has been traced no farther back than this.' *Opposite top right:* The fifth debate between Lincoln and Douglas was held at Galesburg, Illinois, on 7 October 1858. The platform on which they spoke was erected at the east end of Knox College. The students decorated the college with flags, steamers and a large banner bearing the words: 'Knox College for Lincoln.' *Opposite below:* Lincoln the rail splitter. When Lincoln was but eight years old, he had enough strength to swing an ax. *Above:* Lincoln's law office in Springfield, Illinois in 1858 was above the store at the end of the block. As Lincoln was leaving Springfield in 1861 for Washington to be inaugurated, he noticed the sign board at the foot of the steps of this building. It advertised the firm of Lincoln and his partner, William H Herndon. He said: 'Let it hang there undisturbed. Give our clients to understand that the election of a President makes no change in the firm of Lincoln and Herndon.' *Right:* The inauguration of Abraham Lincoln as sixteenth president of the United States – 4 March 1861.

THE SOUTH SECEDES

Southern secession took place in two stages. The lower South, the 'cotton states,' withdrew from the Union in consequence of Lincoln's election; a northern tier, including Virginia, seceded on the question of states rights when President Lincoln resolved to hold the nation together by force. Some border slave states (Delaware, Maryland, Kentucky, Missouri and the mountainous part of Virginia that formed the new state of West Virgina) still held to the Union.

Eleven states formed the new Confederate States of America. They were Virginia, North and South Carolina, Georgia, Alabama, Mississippi, Louisiana, Arkansas, Tennessee, Florida and Texas. The new nation had a population of approximately $5\frac{1}{2}$ million whites and $3\frac{1}{2}$ million slaves. The new constitution was closely modeled on that of the United States, with a more explicit recognition of slavery and states rights, and a few technical improvements in the relation of president to Congress. The flag, known as 'The Stars and Bars', was a newly patterned tricolor of red, white and blue. The more familiar St Andrew's Cross was a battle flag. The capital was established first at Montgomery, Alabama and later at Richmond, Virginia.

Jefferson Davis of Mississippi was the only president, and his entire term was filled with war. He was born in Kentucky, not far from Lincoln's first home, but he moved south instead of north and became the owner of a great plantation. Alexander Stevens of Georgia, at first an opponent of secession, was made vice president.

As the North had a much greater population than the Confederacy, an even greater advantage in industrial wealth and command of the sea, one would have expected an early victory. Actually the war which followed (called in the North 'The Rebellion', and in the South 'The War Between the States' and by the world at large 'The American Civil War') was one of the most closely contested wars in history. The South had a strong military tradition, many able generals and a population accustomed to ride, shoot and live in the open. But the greatest asset on the Confederate side was simply that to win, the South had merely to hold its own; the North had to conquer every part of the Confederacy.

Above: An example of industry in the North – the Colt Firearms Company in Hartford, Connecticut. *Below:* Jefferson Davis and his Cabinet. *Right:* Davis, from Mississippi, was elected President of the Confederate States of America in October 1861. *Opposite:* South Carolina voted an ordinance of secession from the Union, repealing its 1788 ratification of the Constitution 20 December 1860. Between 9 January and 8 June 1861, ten other states followed her.

CHARLESTON
MERCURY

EXTRA:

Passed unanimously at 1.15 o'clock, P. M. December 20th, 1860.

AN ORDINANCE

To dissolve the Union betwec ⸻ ⸻ate of South Carolina and other States united with her under the compact entitled "The Constitution of the United States of America."

We, the People of the State of South Carolina, in Convention assembled, do declare and ordain, and it is hereby declared and ordained,

That the Ordinance adopted by us in Convention, on the twenty-third day of May, in the year of our Lord one thousand seven hundred and eighty-eight, whereby the Constitution of the United States of America was ratified, and also, all Acts and parts of Acts of the General Assembly of this State, ratifying amendments of the said Constitution, are hereby repealed; and that the union now subsisting between South Carolina and other States, under the name of "The United States of America," is hereby dissolved.

THE
UNION
IS
DISSOLVED!

THE DAY OF THE CONFEDERACY

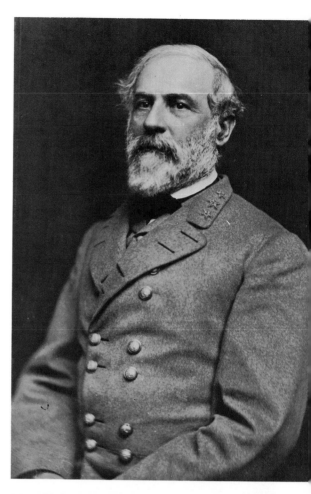

During the first half of the war the Confederacy held the advantage, especially in the East. Robert E Lee, the son of ''Light-Horse Harry' Lee of the Revolution, was a Virginian who did not want secession but thought his primary allegiance was due to his state. He was possibly the ablest general, and certainly the most attractive figure, among the military leaders on either side. It is typical that the North selected a civilian, Lincoln, as its most idolized figure – the South selected Lee, a military hero.

The chief battle of 1861 was at Bull Run (called by the South Manassas) between the two capitals, Washington and Richmond. It was a Confederate victory but not a decisive one. 'Stonewall' Jackson, Lee's ablest general, here gained his nickname by the constancy of his troops. But the Confederates were unable to push on to Washington.

General George McClellan, called to military leadership, was just the man to reorganize the defeated Union army. He was an excellent drillmaster, and too cautious to expose untried troops to battle. But time revealed two defects: he was overcautious, always imagining the foe to be stronger than his own forces, and insubordinate in his attitude toward his civilian superiors. Once he was 'too busy' to see Lincoln, and the patient president said, 'I will hold McClellan's horse if he will bring us victory.'

McClellan had a plan. He wanted to take advantage of the naval superiority of the Union to transport troops to the peninsula in eastern Virginia and to advance toward Richmond, but Confederate strategy forced the withdrawal of Union troops to defend Washington and Richmond was not captured.

Opposite top: Gen Robert E Lee of the Army of the Confederate States of America. Lee was a brilliant tactician and strategist, but he never evolved an overall concept of Southern strategy, partly because the South organized itself into discrete and often non-cooperating military districts. Later in life, Lee came to symbolize the reconciliation of North and South. *Opposite below:* Crew members cooking on the deck of the *Monitor* in the James River 9 July 1862. The *Monitor*, an ironclad, had engaged the *Merrimac*, a Confederate ironclad steam frigate, on 8 March 1862 at Hampton Roads, just off the coast from Norfolk, Virginia. Although outgunned ten to two, the *Monitor* held

its own in the duel. Neither ship was able to do serious damage to the other, but the *Merrimac* withdrew, never again to figure in the war. The engagement did mark a turning point in naval history, since it proved that old-fashioned wooden ships were obsolete. The North later built more ironclads, but the South could not produce another *Merrimac*. *Below:* Allan Pinkerton (smoking a pipe), the chief of Gen George B McClelland's Intelligence Service, with his men near Cumberland County, Virginia 1862. *Overleaf:* One of the major battles of the Peninsular Campaign, the Battle of Williamsburg, cost the Union Forces over 2000 casualties.

Lincoln experimented with other generals – Ambrose Burnside, Pope, and Joseph Hooker. They were less cautious than McClellan and equally successful. Finally he had to recall McClellan to command. Unlike Davis, Lincoln lacked military training and experience, but, whatever his errors in conducting the war, he kept steadily in mind the restoration of the whole Union, and nothing irked him more than generals who were content to limit their vision to the North and say, 'We have repelled the enemy from our soil.'

A new era in naval warfare arrived with the fight between two iron-clad ships, the Confederate *Merrimac* and the Union *Monitor*.

The South won its greatest victory and suffered its greatest loss at Chancellorsville – a victory by Jackson but one which cost him his life. When he first heard that Jackson had lost an arm, Lee said in his gracious way, 'You have lost your left arm; I my right!' This proved to be true. Jackson was perhaps as great a tactician as Lee, although he could never have managed public relations with the temperamental Davis half as well.

Diplomatic difficulties were added to Lincoln's troubles. An American naval officer seized two Confederate agents, Mason and Slidell from the British. The British demanded their surrender and Lincoln wisely acquiesced, saying, 'One war at a time.' Later there was a controversy over the building of Confederate rams in British shipyards. There was much sympathy with the Confederacy in conservative British circles, and a general conviction that the South would win. Napoleon III, the French Emperor, cared nothing about the merits of the war, but he was busy with military plans in Mexico, which a divided United States could not prevent.

Left: Union artillery taking up a position in the Blue Ridge Mountains of Virginia. *Below:* The Confederate army was well positioned in the town and on the heights above Fredericksburg before the Union Forces were deployed. From this impregnable position Lee beat off the rash frontal attack that Gen Ambrose E Burnside launched 13 December 1862. *Opposite below:* A company of Union soldiers photographed during the Sharpsburg campaign. *Overleaf:* The resistance of the Confederate army outside Chattanooga refuted the rumor that they were in retreat. Gen Braxton Bragg had retreated into the city and, when Union Gen William S Rosecrans and his troops advanced on Chattanooga and took the city 9 September 1863, they found that Bragg had entrenched his men in the mountains outside the town. Rosecrans advanced and was badly beaten at Chickamauga 19–20 September and was replaced by Gen George H Thomas.

THE TURN OF THE TIDE

Slavery had caused the war, but the issue on which it was fought was secession. Lincoln wished to emancipate the slaves, but many were held in the Union slave states and he did not want to lose the support of these states. So he discountenanced General Frémont's attempts to confiscate slaves as 'contraband of war.' Abolitionists angrily gibed: 'Lincoln would *like* to have God on his side, but he *must* have Kentucky.'

He had to consider the foreign situation also. In general, Europeans cared little, one way or the other, about secession, but they disliked slavery. If Lincoln could tie the two issues together he could safely issue an emancipation proclamation. William Seward, his Secretary of State, advised him to wait for some military success and 'issue it with victory.' The chance came when McClellan stopped Lee in Maryland at the battle of Antietam (or Sharpsburg). So Lincoln declared that if the Confederate states were still in rebellion by January, 1863 their slaves would be freed.

Literally this did not free a single slave. It did not apply to the Union slave states and the Confederacy, of course, refused to recognize Lincoln's authority. But it doomed slavery unless the Confederacy won, for it committed the Union government to emancipation.

Also, 1863 was the military turn of the tide. Lee invaded Pennsylvania and was met by General George Meade at Gettysburg. In a three day battle in July the Confederates were compelled to retreat.

Vicksburg, the last holdout of the Confederates on the Mississippi River, was taken in the same month by General Ulysses S Grant, a Mexican war veteran. This led to Grant's eventual command of the chief Union forces.

And yet the war was only half over. For many months the Confederates stubbornly held out. There was more discouragement in the North in 1864 than among all the defeats of 1862, and Lincoln himself thought that he might not be re-elected. The Democrats nominated General McClellan and many Republicans (how strange it sounds now) demanded a 'stronger' candidate. If General William Tecumseh Sherman had not, in the nick of time, won some striking victories in the South, Lincoln's fears might have been warranted. But he won handily (the South, of course, not voting) and said that the voters evidently thought it best 'not to swap horses while crossing a stream.'

Above: Artillery about to go into action on the south bank of the Rappahannock River in Virginia 4 June 1863. *Opposite:* The Palmetto Battery in Charleston, South Carolina 1863. *Right:* A view of the Battle of Gettysburg on 2 July 1863. That day Gen James Longstreet's corps marched the full length of the battlefield in the hope of surprising the Union defense – to no avail. At Gettysburg Lee was hampered by the half-hearted cooperation of Longstreet, who did not believe that Lee should take the offensive in that battle. *Overleaf:* Gen William T Sherman's advance toward Atlanta was temporarily halted at the Battle of Kenesaw Mountain where the Army of Tennessee was firmly entrenched.

Above: Four Union generals who were present at Gettybsburg. Seated is Maj Gen Winfield Scott Hancock. Standing, left to right, are Maj Gen David Birney, Brig Gen Francis Barlow and Brig Gen John Gibbon. *Far left:* Gen William Tecumseh Sherman in 1865. *Left:* Gen Ulysses Simpson Grant, the military hero of the Union forces. *Opposite top:* A rare photograph of Vicksburg, Mississippi taken in 1863 during the siege. Vickburg was the most serious obstacle to northern control of the Mississippi River and was defended by Gen J C Pemberton. The siege lasted from 17 May to 4 July, when Pemberton surrendered to Grant. *Opposite below:* The Union losses at Gettysburg were about 23,000 compared to the Confederate death toll of approximately 30,000.

TRIUMPH AND TRAGEDY

In the eastern theater Grant and Lee met in a series of battles. In the West, General Thomas defeated General John Hood. In the South, Sherman marched through Georgia 'from Atlanta to the sea' and then into South Carolina. At long last, Lee surrendered at Appomatox Court House, which practically ended the war.

Lincoln's second inaugural address, with victory in sight, held out a promise of reconciliation to the South. In Congress he opposed the vindictiveness of the congressmen's attitude, and proposed reconstruction, state by state, as soon as ten percent of the voters were willing to take an oath of allegiance.

His conciliatory plans were defeated by his death. While he was at ease in his box in Ford's Theater in Washington, the box was entered by a fanatical actor, John Wilkes Booth, who shot him. The assassin leaped to the stage, injuring his leg, and shouting, 'Sic semper tyrannis! The South is avenged!' Booth was eventually hunted down and shot and a few fellow conspirators tried and executed.

Mourning in the North was general, but the greatest injury had been inflicted on the South. Vice president Andrew Johnson, who now became president, was a Union Democrat from Tennessee. He honestly intended to carry out Lincoln's conciliatory policies, but he had neither Lincoln's tact nor the prestige of being the 'man who won the war.' His chief opposition came, not from the Democrats, but from radical Republicans who wanted to reconstruct the South on a basis of equal rights for the freedman.

By the three 'Civil War Amendments' (the 13th, 14th and 15th), the former slaves were everywhere given freedom, then civil rights and finally the suffrage.

Troops in the trenches at Petersburg, Virginia in 1865. The siege of that town lasted from the summer of 1864 until 2 April 1865. *Left:* Grant had arrived at Petersburg in June 1864. The Union attacks had failed and Grant settled down to siege and trench warfare.

Left: The Andersonville Prison Camp in 1865. This Confederate prison in Georgia consisted of a log stockade through which ran a small stream. In an area of only 26 acres the number of prisoners often rose to over 30,000. Poor food, bad sanitary conditions and exposure took a toll of some 13,000 known dead – the grand total was probably higher. *Opposite below:* The building at Appomattox Court House, Virginia where Lee and Grant met 9 April 1865 and Lee surrendered his command of the Army of Northern Virginia. *Right:* The victorious Union army returning home in triumph. *Below:* The assassination of Abraham Lincoln five days after the end of the war opened the harsh era of Reconstruction. Had Lincoln lived, there is reason to believe that the United States would have been spared much of the bitterness that was a legacy of the war.

PART 3
THE INDUSTRIAL REVOLUTION AND WORLD POWER, 1866-1918

Naturally, the immediate problems after the Civil War were reconstruction of the South. But these issues soon gave way to economic ones: the tariff, the currency question, the grievances of labor and the problems of the farmer.

In 1876 the Democrats almost won the presidency, and in 1884 succeeded with the election of Grover Cleveland. For a time there was a third party agrarian movement, the Populists, who protested against eastern capitalism. In 1896 it coalesced with the Democrats.

With the new century, Populism faded, but the reform movement did not. Theodore Roosevelt, the Republican, and Woodrow Wilson, the Democrat, gave new impulse to political changes such as the popular election of senators, direct primaries and equal suffrage for women. Still more evident was a demand for economic reforms, curbing the trusts, conserving natural resources and legislation benefitting labor.

With the Spanish-American War of 1898 and the acquisition of a small colonial empire, the United States became recognized as one of the 'Great Powers.' Although President Roosevelt waged no wars, he made American influence felt by vigorous diplomatic initiatives. During Wilson's administration, war broke out in Europe in 1914 and involved the United States in 1917. In the following year a great coalition of nations defeated Germany and her allies.

'Smoke means prosperity
in steel': Pittsburgh 1909.

RECONSTRUCTION YEARS: JOHNSON AND GRANT

Reconstruction had three meanings. One, of course, was the physical rehabilitation of a war-torn section of the country. Another was the restoration of the seceding states to their full place in the Union. But the third, the most difficult and significant, was the adjustment of racial relations between the white southerners and their former slaves.

President Andrew Johnson put little emphasis on this last. He was a Unionist, but also a southerner, and he thought that, once the slaves were emancipated, they could be safely left to the individual states. Radical Republicans feared that this would mean the establishment of a kind of general serfdom and second-class citizenship for the former slaves. They established a 'Freedman's Bureau' to handle racial issues and insisted on equal suffrage.

One reason why this was politically important was that the electoral vote of the South would be increased, since slaves counted for only 3/5 as much as freemen in apportionment, and there were no slaves.

The radical Republicans also tried to curb Johnson's power with a Tenure of Office Act, by which the consent of the Senate was required for removals from (as well as appointments to) federal office.

When Johnson violated this law by removing Edwin Stanton from the War Department, the House of Representatives impeached him, and the Senate acted as a court to try the case. A 2/3 verdict is required in such cases. The Democrats voted solidly for Johnson and they were joined by seven Republicans who, though they did not like Johnson, thought that the Tenure of Office Act was unwarranted by the Constitution. Since then,

Left: Following the war, Normal Schools were set up in the South for the education of former slaves. Lucy (front center) and Sarah Chase (front left) worked for the Freedmen's Bureau and are shown with a group of Normal School teachers at or near Norfolk, Virginia in 1865. *Opposite bottom:* A scene in Richmond, Virginia after the evacuation of the Confederate troops in that city 1 April 1865. *Right:* A vicious poster deriding the activities of the Freedmen's Bureau. *Below:* The Freedmen's Bureau was a national agency created in March 1865 to provide relief and guidance for blacks and other refugees who had concentrated around the army camps and in the southern towns and cities.

THE FREEDMAN'S BUREAU!

AN AGENCY TO KEEP THE NEGRO IN IDLENESS AT THE EXPENSE OF THE WHITE MAN.
TWICE VETOED BY THE PRESIDENT, AND MADE A LAW BY CONGRESS.

SUPPORT CONGRESS & YOU SUPPORT THE NEGRO.   SUSTAIN THE PRESIDENT & YOU PROTECT THE WHITE MAN

For 1864 and 1865, the FREEDMAN'S BUREAU cost the Tax-payers of the Nation, at least, TWENTY-FIVE MILLIONS OF DOLLARS.   For 1866, THE SHARE of the Tax-payers of Pennsylvania will be about ONE MILLION OF DOLLARS.   GEARY is FOR the Freedman's Bureau.   CLYMER is OPPOSED to it.

137

no president has been impeached.

Grant sided with the reconstructionist Republicans. He had never hitherto taken any interest in politics, but his military prestige enabled him to gain an easy victory over Governor Seymour of New York.

The new administration had some successes. It restored financial credit and, with the able Secretary of State, Hamilton Fish, arbitrated outstanding claims against Great Britain. But Grant's political inexperience was evident in many of his appointments. Personally honest, he was too loyal to unworthy friends. Graft was discovered in postal and Indian reservation contracts and in the licensing of distilleries. A Liberal Republican reform movement sought an alternative to Grant in 1872. Unfortunately they chose as their candidate Horace Greeley, an editor of genius, but erratic and unstable. As one historian put it, 'the man of no ideas was running against the man with too many.' Grant was easily victorious.

The executive branch was not alone in being tainted. Many congressmen had accepted bribes from railway companies. Local government in the South was wielded by northern 'carpetbaggers' (as if all their wealth were held in one carpet bag). In New York City the Tweed Ring, supported by Tammany Hall, plundered the city of many millions of dollars.

138

ATE
President
EARER
1868
Brown
ergeant-at-Arms.

Left: A facsimile of a ticket of admission to the impeachment trial of President Andrew Johnson. *Opposite below:* The managers of the House of Representatives at the impeachment of Johnson. Standing left to right: James F Wilson (Iowa), George S Boutwell (Massachusetts), John A Logan (Illinois). Seated left to right: Benjamin F Butler (Massachusetts), Thaddeus Stevens (Pennsylvania), Thomas Williams (Pennsylvania), John A Bingham (Ohio). *Below:* Andrew Johnson. *Right:* Thaddeus Stevens and John A Bingham before the Senate. *Below center:* Ulysses S Grant. *Below right:* Hamilton Fish, Grant's second Secretary of State.

HARPER'S WEEKLY.
A JOURNAL OF CIVILIZATION

VOL. XII.—No. 585.]   NEW YORK, SATURDAY, MARCH 14, 1868.   [SINGLE COPIES, TEN CENTS. $4.00 PER YEAR IN ADVANCE.

Entered according to Act of Congress, in the Year 1868, by Harper & Brothers, in the Clerk's Office of the District Court of the United States, for the Southern District of New York.

AMERICAN SCIENCE AND INVENTION

The contributions of the United States to applied science have been as numerous and important as those of any nation. This is especially true in the fields of rapid transportation and communications. Robert Fulton's steamboat (1803), Samuel Morse's telegraph (1837), Field's Atlantic cable (1866), Alexander Graham Bell's telephone (1876) were significant steps for a nation 'always in a hurry.' Though the steam locomotive was a British invention and the automobile owed much to the German internal combustion engine, they attained their widest use in America, and the first successful airplane flight was made by the Wright Brothers in North Carolina in 1903.

The work of Thomas Edison contributed largely to the phonograph, the motion picture and the electric light. In all, he took out more than a thousand patents.

Agricultural machines, such as the cotton gin, the reapers, binders and harvesters, owe much to American inventors. The shortage of domestic servants increased reliance on mechanisms in the home, such as sewing machines, refrigerators, vacuum cleaners and dishwashing machines. Office work profited from American elevators, typewriters, cash registers and calculating machines.

But in so-called 'pure science' it was hardly before the 20th century that America seriously competed with Europe. The advance of American science in recent generations is evident in the number of Nobel Prizes that they have won.

An example of American achievement in medicine was the discovery by a team of experimenters under Walter Reed that yellow fever was carried by the bite of a mosquito. As a result, this disease was eliminated from Cuba and the Panama Canal Zone, which facilitated the construction of the canal.

Left: Thomas Alva Edison experimenting with micrography in his New Jersey laboratory. The holder of more than 1000 patents, this great American inventor was a pioneer in many fields, including electric illumination, the motion pictures, and the phonograph. *Top:* Samuel F B Morse, a professor at the University of the City of New York, invented the telegraph and sent his first news message from Washington to Annapolis 1 May 1844. *Above:* Edison with his 'talking machine.' *Opposite top left:* The Paris Exposition of 1900 featured the first step-type escalator ever to be installed. *Opposite top right:* A sample elevator manufactured about 1896. *Right:* In 1910 John Kowalski, a marine engine maker, built this aircraft. Its test flight near Aspinwall, Pennsylvania ended in a crash.

Opposite top: A wheat thresher of about 1802. It was powered by sweep horsepower and could thresh some 200–300 bushels of wheat per day. *Opposite bottom:* The Case 80 horsepower steam tractor. *Above:* Robert Fulton's *Clermont*. Fulton made the first practical steamboat trip on this vessel, leaving New York City 17 August 1807 and arriving at Albany, New York, a distance of 150 miles, in 32 hours. *Right:* Building the Panama Canal in 1907. The building of the canal was a huge engineering feat.

THE ERA OF BIG BUSINESS

In the days before the Civil War, ambitious youths dreamed of being president, or at least a senator; in the generation after it they were more apt to dream of becoming business tycoons. Politics was still, perhaps, the favorite national sport but most people would have agreed with the later dictum of President Calvin Coolidge: 'The business of America is business!'

Particularly important was the rapid development of railroad transportation. The Union Pacific Railroad completed its tracks across the continent. Cornelius Vanderbilt, James Hill, William Harriman and Leland Stanford, the railroad builders, changed American life as profoundly as any of the politicians.

Since it is impossible to tell the whole story of the American industrial revolution, we may select as typical the careers of John D Rockefeller and Andrew Carnegie. Both men rose from humble beginnings. Rockefeller began with a petty local business; Carnegie was a poor boy who emigrated from Scotland.

In time, Rockefeller was able to organize most of the petroleum industry with his Standard Oil Company and its many branches. He was deemed the wealthiest man in the world. It is estimated that he gave 600 million dollars away in philanthropy, including 35 million to the University of Chicago.

In similar fashion, Carnegie organized the iron and steel industry. He, too, endowed education in both Scotland and America and specialized in the erection of libraries. He also built a Peace Palace for the Hague Court.

The multimillionaires did not escape criticism. The consolidated trust companies (the 'trusts') forced many rival firms out of business and sometimes almost monopolized a whole industry. The railroads often exacted from shippers 'all that the traffic would bear.' Moreover, not all businessmen were constructive industrialists; some, such as Jay Gould, Fisk and Drew were merely fortunate gamblers, skimming the cream from other men's milk.

Above: E W Harriman, who brought the Union Pacific and the Southern Pacific Railroads together in 1900. *Below:* A cartoon of the time, *The Bosses of the Senate* showing the various big trusts taking over the law-making function. *Opposite top left:* A poster announcing the opening of the railroad line from Omaha to San Francisco 10 May 1869. *Opposite* *top right:* Following the Civil War, the railroads came into their own. Oil transportation by the Oil Creek Valley Railroad, near Roweville, Pennsylvania, about 1868. *Opposite bottom left:* Cornelius Vanderbilt, the owner of the New York Central and the Hudson River Railroads. *Opposite bottom right:* Construction Camp, Central Pacific Railroad, 1869.

Above: Andrew Carnegie, the Scottish immigrant who was brought to America at the age of 13 and first worked in a cotton factory for S1.20 per week. He later became a telegraph operator and then the private secretary of a Pennsylvania Railroad official. From railroading he went to bridge building. In 1873 he opened his first steel mill. Later he gave millions to good works, including schools and libraries.
Right: Steel towns at the turn of the century were most unpleasant – a view of the mills and the homes of workers in Pittsburg, 1909.

GERMAN AND IRISH IMMIGRATION

From the 1840s until about 1890 the chief immigration had been from Germany and southern Ireland. The causes must be sought in Europe. The failure of the German revolution of 1848 sent many liberals to the United States. The bulk of German emigration, however, was caused by economics. The population of Germany was rapidly increasing, and not all could find profitable employment in the Fatherland. When German industry developed sufficiently, the emigration suddenly stopped.

In the case of the Irish, the main cause was the potato failure and consequent famine. There had been earlier Irish immigration, but it had been chiefly of the Scotch-Irish from Protestant Ulster. The new tide was mainly Roman Catholic. This stirred the fires of religious bigotry. Some business firms put out signs, 'Help wanted, but no Irish need apply'. In the 1850s there was a short-lived anti-Catholic American Party, commonly called the 'Know Nothings' because they met in secret conclave and instructed their adherents to profess ignorance of the organization.

The Irish settled mainly in the big cities of the Northeast, especially Boston and New York, where they came to have great political influence. The Germans, as a rule, moved farther west to such cities as Cincinnati, St Louis and Milwaukee. Since many of these were Protestants, they met with less hostility, though some Americans professed to fear 'German Socialism.'

Above: Many of the Irish immigrants came to the United States on vessels such as the *Liverpool.* In the etching the transatlantic steamship is shown on her first voyage to New York City in October 1838. *Opposite top:* Irish immigrants about to leave their homes for America. The mail coach is about to depart from Cahirciveen, County Kerry, Ireland for the port where their ship awaits. *Opposite below:* One of the earliest pictures of Irish immigrants in steerage, from the *Illustrated London News* 10 May 1851. The accompanying article gave a small idea of the vast numbers of Irish who left for America. 'I find that during the week ending April 11 the greatest rush for the season took place. The numbers who left Cork that week could not have fallen far short of 1500 souls, and this with the emigration of the other ports of Limerick, Waterford, Dublin, and even of Belfast, will give us an approach to 5000 weekly leaving the country. Large as this number may appear, it is well known that it is considerably below the mark when the departures for Liverpool are included. One agent informed me that he himself had booked 600 emigrants in four days, and yet he is but one of the many who are to be met with not alone in the large towns and seaports, but scattered through each petty town and village throughout the country.'

149

Opposite: Early immigrants to New York were grouped together in the Emigrant Landing Depot at Castle Garden. Ellis Island was not opened until 1891. *Top: Landing Immigrants at Castle Garden,* from *Harper's Magazine* June 1884. *Above:* Registering the names of immigrants at Castle Garden Receiving Station in New York. Many of these people had their names permanently changed because the immigration officials were unable to cope with unfamiliar foreign spellings (from *Harper's Monthly* 1870).

THE CENTENNIAL YEAR

Opposite: A photograph of the Republican National Convention in Chicago 2 June 1880. *Above left:* Rutherford B Hayes, the nineteenth president of the United States. *Above right:* Samuel J Tilden, who lost to Hayes in 'The Disputed Election.'

In 1876 both parties put up able candidates. The Democrats selected Samuel Tilden, a reformer and New York governor; the Republicans nominated Rutherford B Hayes, the governor of Ohio. The economic depression of 1873 and the scandals of Grant's administration gave the Democrats hope. The result of the election hung in dispute on the vote of three states, Florida, Louisiana and South Carolina. The Democrats had the popular plurality in the nation as a whole and charged that carpetbag administrations in these states were falsifying the returns. The Republicans retorted that Ku Klux Klan terrorism had prevented many former slaves from casting their lawful votes.

A special electoral commission, drawn from the House, the Senate and the Supreme Court, was asked to adjudicate the rival claims. By a partisan margin of eight to seven the election was awarded to Hayes by a single electoral vote. Historians still debate who really won.

Hayes removed federal troops from the parts of the South where they were still stationed. He tried to control the excesses of the spoils system, but the shadow of uncertainty which hung over his election hampered him, and he did not seek a second term.

In 1880, partisans of General Grant tried to get him a third term. James G Blaine, the most prominent Republican leader, also reached for the nomination. The convention finally turned to a compromise candidate, James A Garfield of Ohio. The Democrats nominated General Scott Hancock, a Union officer, but personally popular in the South. Garfield was elected, but was shot by a disappointed office-seeker, and Vice President Chester A Arthur became president.

Four years later the Democrats had their first postwar presidential success. They nominated Grover Cleveland, the governor of New York, a reformer and an opponent of Tammany Hall, the New York City political machine. The Republicans chose Blaine. The campaign which followed was one of the closest – and dirtiest – in American history. Since the parties had no clear issue between them, the struggle turned on personalities. Blaine was accused of using his political clout to advance his private railway speculations; Cleveland was accused of having an illegitimate child.

What tipped the balances was a close majority for Cleveland in New York. Blaine had allowed himself to attend a fund raising banquet of rich men ('Belshazzar's Feast' the Democrats called it) and had overlooked a careless phrase of the Reverend Burchard, who said that the Democratic Party was one of 'Rum, Romanism and Rebellion.' Rebellion meant the South, rum the liquor interests and both were already safely Democratic; but Romanism was taken as an insult by many Republican Catholics, who promptly shifted to Cleveland.

153

Cleveland tried to curb the rush for political spoils and vetoed many private pension bills which he considered unwarranted. He ran the election of 1888 on the tariff issue, favoring 'a tariff for revenue only', while his opponent, Benjamin Harrison, the grandson of old 'Tippecanoe,' championed protection. Harrison won a single term, but was defeated by Cleveland in 1892.

During the whole period from 1876 to 1892 inclusive, the two parties were of approximate strength. Both were essentially conservative, so radical discontent had to find embodiment in third party movements. Chief among these was the People's Party, commonly called the Populists, strongest in the grain-growing prairie states. To explain it, we must consider the economic conditions in that area.

Below: James A Garfield, the twentieth president of the United States, was shot in Washington DC, 2 July 1881, and died of his wounds 19 September. This etching from *Frank Leslie's Illustrated Newspaper* 16 July 1881 bore the caption 'Washington D C – The Attack on the President's Life – Mrs Smith Supporting the President While Awaiting the Arrival of the Ambulance. *Opposite:* The National Democratic Chart for 1876.

THE DAY OF THE COWBOY

After the Civil War there was a surplus of beef cattle in western Texas. Therefore many drovers sent herds north to shipping points in Kansas and Nebraska. At that time the prairie country was mostly open range and there was nothing to stop the cattle drives. The last important Indian battle in the North was Sitting Bull's massacre of a force of soldiers under the command of General George Custer, a Civil War veteran, in 1876. Thereafter nearly all Indians were forced into special reservations.

The equipment of the cowboy was derived from the similar *vaquero* of Mexico: broad-brimmed hat (the sombrero) for shade from the sun, leggings (chaps) to safeguard his legs in riding in rough country, jingling spurs and a coiled rope to catch stray cattle. To prevent the mixing of herds, cattle were branded with the mark of their owners. Persons caught stealing cattle or altering brands were often shot or hanged on sight.

The cowboy has been a romantic figure in novels, plays and motion pictures, but essentially he was an ordinary young man, methodically earning his way in the cattle business as did his grandfather in the Massachusetts cod fisheries or his grandson working in a service station. He was bothered not only by rustlers, or cattle thieves, but also by sheep herders whose flocks cropped the grass too closely for cattle to follow, and, most of all by farmers whose barbed wire fences broke the open range.

There are still many beef cattle, but the open range has gone; fenced ranches have taken its place. Some ranches have turned into holiday recreation centers, or 'dude ranches' – 'dude' meaning any tourist from the east.

Left below: Gen George Armstrong Custer. *Below:* The Battle of the Little Big Horn.

Left: A Montana Indian cowboy. *Right:* Cowboys sitting around the chuckwagon eating a meal. The chuckwagon was invented by the cattle king Charles Goodnight as a device to serve as a traveling kitchen for his cowboys while they were on a cattle drive. An army wagon was adapted for the purpose, and was fitted with a upright 'chuck' or kitchen box at the rear. The chuck box contained compartments to hold provisions and utensils and its tailgate door dropped down to form a table on which the cook would work. The chuckwagon carried a water barrel, wood for the fire, the crew's bedrolls and other equipment. *Below:* The temporary cattle roundup town of Lone Cove, Colorado near the Wyoming border. This area was run primarily by the Warren Cattle Company, and these are probably Warren's employees and cattle.

THE FARMERS' PROTEST

The settlement of the prairie country in Oklahoma, Kansas, Nebraska, the Dakotas and the eastern parts of Colorado, Wyoming and Montana presented very different problems from those encountered by the pioneers of the old Northwest. Settlers did not have to cut down trees and root out their stumps, but on the other hand, they lacked lumber to build their houses and barns. Droughts were frequent, snowstorms and hailstorms severe and tornadoes so common that many farmers dug cyclone cellars for shelter in an emergency.

They also had economic difficulties. Many farms were heavily mortgaged. The interest on these was easily paid in good years, but the climate was fickle and in lean years they constituted a serious burden. The railways were the farmers' only means of reaching eastern markets and so freight rates were a common grievance.

For their common protection, the farmers formed granges, 'Patrons of Husbandry,' 'greenback movements' (payment of debts in paper currency) and other associations, which eventually coalesced into the Populist movement. The Populist demanded 'free and unlimited coinage of silver' so that they could pay their debts in a cheaper coinage than gold. In addition, they demanded government regulation of freight rates, and sometimes went so far as to favor government ownership of railways, telegraphs and telephones.

But they were not Socialists. American Socialism was essentially urban and to a great extent imported from Europe; Populism was native and rural. In 1892 they carried some electoral votes and won support, not only from the wheat and corn belts, but also from the silver mining states in the Rocky Mountains.

Ho for Kansas!

Brethren, Friends, & Fellow Citizens:

I feel thankful to inform you that the

REAL ESTATE

AND

Homestead Association,

Will Leave Here the

15th of April, 1878,

In pursuit of Homes in the Southwestern Lands of America, at Transportation Rates, cheaper than ever was known before.

For full information inquire of

Benj. Singleton, better known as old Pap,

NO. 5 NORTH FRONT STREET.

Beware of Speculators and Adventurers, as it is a dangerous thing to fall in their hands.

Nashville, Tenn., March 18, 1878.

Above: A call for blacks to leave Tennessee and move to Kansas. *Below:* A family poses beside their covered wagon in the Loup Valley of Central Nebraska. The year is 1886. *Opposite top:* A photograph taken of a Shoshone irrigation project 6 October 1904 set up on Shoshone farmlands near Cody, Wyoming. *Opposite bottom:* The small town of Guernsey, Wyoming. Here, travelers would be offered only liquid refreshment. *Overleaf:* A farmhouse near Aberdeen, South Dakota in 1882.

PIONEER

E IN 1882

Left: A post office in the
vicinity of Coburgh,
Nebraska photographed
about 1887. Below: Not all
the homesteaders were
white Anglo-Saxon types.
The Shores family
homesteaded near
Westerville, Custer
County, Nebraska in 1887.
Opposite top: The Holland
& McDonald hardware
store in Coburgh,
Nebraska in 1887. Note
the signs for Deere
Harvesting Machinery
and Studebaker Wagons.
Opposite bottom: After the
Oklahoma Territory was
opened to homesteaders
22 April 1889, it was
sometimes necessary to
camp on a land claim in
order to hold it, as these
people near Guthrie,
Oklahoma did in 1889.

THE ELECTION OF 1896

Certain presidential elections are landmarks. Such were 1800, which brought Jefferson to power; 1828, which did the same for Jackson; and 1860, which brought on a civil war. Among these we must add 1896.

The Republicans had little internal difficulty. With the expert aid of his friend, Mark Hanna, the Ohio protectionist, Congressman William McKinley, was nominated with only token opposition. The Democratic Party had been snatched from the conservative Grover Cleveland, and the convention was swayed by the oratory of William Jennings Bryan, a young congressman from Nebraska. In a debate on the currency issue, Bryan had thundered, 'You shall not press down upon the brow of labor this crown of thorns; you shall not crucify mankind upon a cross of gold!' This speech secured his nomination.

William McKinley would have preferred a fight on the familiar ground of tariff protection, but the currency issue captured everybody's attention. The Democratic and Populist cry of 'bi-metalism at a ratio of 16 to 1' really meant a silver standard, since the actual value of gold was then over 30 to 1 and debtors found it more convenient to pay in silver, the depressed metal. The Republicans were forced to champion the gold standard. This caused secessions in both parties. A few Republicans from the West supported Bryan, whereas the gold Democrats attempted to form a new third party. The Populists joined Bryan.

The very hot campaign which followed was one of the 'haves' against the 'have nots'. The Democrats swept the South and the trans-Mississippi West; the Republicans won with the East and Middle West. Mark Hanna campaigned on the issue of prosperity. Not only the business community, but also many of the farmers and workingmen in eastern states feared Bryan's radicalism and hoped that the Republican victory would mean better times.

Above: A cartoon from the *New York Journal* 4 August 1896 showing the hand of Mark Hanna supporting the Syndicate by a chain. The title was *A Man of Mark! Left:* The Republican National Convention 18 June 1896. *Opposite top:* William McKinley, the twenty-fifth president of the United States. *Right:* A cartoon of William Jennings Bryan after his 'Cross of Gold' speech. Entitled *The Sacrilegious Candidate,* it carried the statement 'No Man Who Drags in the Dust the Most Sacred Symbols of the Christian World is Fit to Be President of the United States.' It appeared in *Judge* magazine 19 September 1896. *Far right:* Marcus Alonzo 'Mark' Hanna.

Left: The National Democratic Convention of 1900. *Below:* William Jennings Bryan addressing the convention. *Opposite:* A campaign poster of Bryan.

THE NEW IMMIGRATION

From 1890 onward, and increasing up to the First World War, immigration came largely from southern and eastern Europe. The Slavs, Hungarians and southern Italians were mainly seeking a better livelihood. The Russian Jews also had the motive of racial and religious persecution under the Tsar's government. Some Armenians fled from even more cruel mistreatment in Turkey. In the first decade of the 20th century nearly 9 million immigrants entered the United States.

Naturally, this caused some misgivings. Laws were passed against the entry of anarchists, polygamists, persons with certain diseases, persons likely to become paupers and contract laborers. Already Chinese labor, which had led to racial strife on the Pacific coast, had been banned.

In Woodrow Wilson's time, Congress had attempted to bar illiterates, but the president, considering this more a test of opportunity than of ability, had vetoed the plan. It was not until after the First World War that any numerical limitation was attempted. The Japanese objected to being classed with the Chinese, and President Roosevelt made a gentleman's agreement by which the Japanese themselves agreed to restrict labor emigration.

The results of the new immigration were mixed. The Slavs did some of the hardest and heaviest work in the mills and mines. The Jews were successful in the clothing industry, in retail business generally and in the professions. The Italians were frugal, cheerful and hard-working. But massive illiteracy and poverty had a depressing effect on native American labor and, apart from quality, the sheer quantity of the new immigration caused problems of assimilation.

Below left: A cartoon by Thomas Nast showing a Chinese coolie being protected from a mob by the Spirit of Liberty. The Chinese had entered California during the gold rush days. During the Depression of the 1870s, the attitude toward them turned hostile, since they were considered cheap labor. In 1882 the Chinese Exclusion Act regulating immigration was passed. *Below:* Immigrants coming to the United States aboard the SS *Westernland* about 1890. *Right:* The immigration landing station at Ellis Island in New York Harbor 1905. *Far right below:* Italian immigrants landing at Ellis Island in 1905.

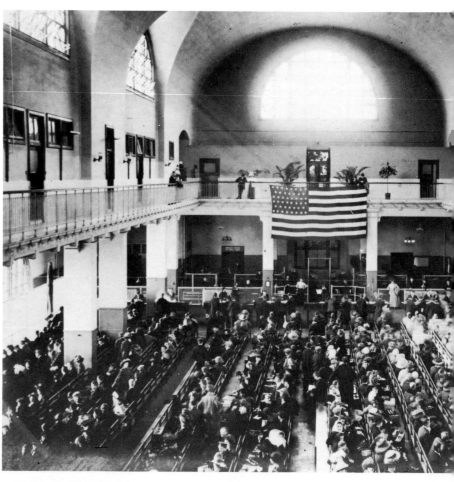

Far left top: Dutch children at Ellis Island. *Above:* The Registry Hall at Ellis Island in 1911. It was large enough to hold 5000 immigrants at once. *Far left:* An Albanian woman at Ellis Island in 1905. *Left:* Romanians at Ellis Island wearing their native costumes. *Right:* An Armenian Jewish immigrant at Ellis Island, 1926. *Overleaf:* Many of the Jewish immigrants moved immediately to the Lower East Side of Manhattan, where conditions were extremely crowded.

Left: A New York City judge swearing in new citizens 8 February 1916. *Below:* Slavic immigrants in New York were often crowded into tenement buildings. *Right:* Immigrants often made the most patriotic citizens. Elementary school children saluting the flag in the Mott Street Industrial School on Manhattan's Lower East Side, 1889. *Opposite below:* Meanwhile, as Thomas Nast pointed out in his cartoon, Native Americans were being denied the vote that was freely given to naturalized American men. The illustration carries the caption 'Has the Native American No Rights That the Naturalized American Is Bound to Respect?'

THE SPANISH WAR

Small wars often have great effects. The McKinley administration had been elected on purely domestic issues, but ex-President Cleveland warned McKinley that the Cuban question was likely to become acute. It had long been a sore spot to the United States. Even before the Civil War, the South had viewed Cuba with covetous eyes as a possible future slave state. The Cubans themselves were dissatisfied and, in a ten years' war (1868–78) kept up a native rebellion. American sympathies were involved and a few American volunteers engaged in the conflict. War broke out again in the 1890s.

Congress was bent on war, and McKinley yielded. Spain was of herding the people into concentration camps. Interventionist newspapers, vying for circulation, kept the excitement at fever heat. The climax was reached when the American battleship *Maine* was blown up in the harbor of Havana. An American committee of investigation showed that the explosion had some external cause, but no one knows for certain whether this was a Spanish torpedo or an accidental collision with a mine. A great cry arose: 'Remember the *Maine*!'

Congress was not bent on war, and McKinley yielded. Spain was ordered out of Cuba and, when it delayed, war followed. Commodore George Dewey was ordered to send the Asiatic fleet to the Spanish Philippines. He smashed the Spanish fleet in Manila Bay. Cuba, Puerto Rico and the Philippines, all fell into American hands. Independently of the war, the United States annexed the Hawaiian Islands on their own petition.

Bryan, although still clinging to 'free silver', said that imperialism was the 'paramount issue'. He advocated immediate independence for the Philippines. McKinley thought the Filipinos unready for independence. As the United States had done after the Mexican War, it paid a sum for the annexed islands. The Americans evacuated Cuba and made Puerto Rico and Hawaii territories, but kept the Philippines in a temporary colonial status. The American public was happily expansionist, and McKinley was duly re-elected in 1900.

There was a temporary boom for George Dewey, now an admiral, for president, but it came to nothing. The only real crisis in the 1900 election was the selection of Theodore Roosevelt for vice president. He had served with a cavalry regiment of 'Rough Riders' and had been elected governor of New York. Western sentiment insisted on his nomination and Boss Platt of New York favored it because Roosevelt was too independent of party discipline in the state. Mark Hanna dreaded it. 'Now it is up to you to live,' he told McKinley.

Above: The battleship *Maine* was destroyed in Havana Harbor 15 February 1898 with a heavy loss of life. The *Maine* had been sent to Cuba in January 1898 to protect American citizens and interests in the area. The United States believed that Spain was responsible for the sabotage. *Below:* Adm George Dewey, the hero of Manila Bay. *Right:* The Great White Fleet steaming into San Francisco Harbor, 1908. *Below right:* American troops guarding insurgent prisoners in Havana.

Left: Theodore 'Teddy' Roosevelt with some of his troops after the battle at San Juan, 1898. Roosevelt, who had resigned his post as an Assistant Secretary of the Navy to accept a commission as an Army lieutenant colonel, formed his 'Rough Riders,' a regiment of cowboy cavalry recruited principally from Arizona, New Mexico, Texas and the Indian Territory. On 1 July 1898 they took part in a famous action to take the San Juan Heights, a fortified ridge near Santiago. They took Kettle Hill, a height separate from the main ridge. Almost overnight Roosevelt became a national hero. *Right:* Hawaii seemed to be an ideal spot for a mid-Pacific base following Dewey's triumph at Manila Bay. Congress passed an annexation bill, and a ceremony was held in Honolulu celebrating the annexation. *Below:* California and Idaho troops camping in a churchyard at San Pedro, Mocoti, after the Spanish-American War, 1899.

THE REPUBLICAN ROOSEVELT

While McKinley was attending an exposition at Buffalo a man with a bandaged hand approached him. Under the bandage was a revolver. He shot the president, who died a few days later. Mark Hanna's nightmare had come true: 'that cowboy' had become president.

Theodore Roosevelt, the youngest man ever to become president, had a youthful energy and ambition. His Old Dutch family was wealthy enough for him to have lived a life of comfortable leisure, but he preferred activity. No man had ever a more varied career. He had been a rancher, soldier, author, civil service administrator, police commissioner, naval officer, governor of New York and, reluctantly, vice president. He was interested in everything and especially in political reform.

He promised, sincerely enough, to follow in the footsteps of McKinley and carry out his policies, but his temperament prevented him from being the same kind of president. McKinley was an intelligent, dignified, kindly man, but one who rather followed than led Congress and public opinion. Roosevelt shared McKinley's Republicanism. He despised Bryan personally and although, as a 'Mugwump', he had fought against Blaine's nomination in 1884, he remained loyal to his party. But the resemblance ended there.

In domestic matters, Roosevelt pressed on Congress railroad freight rate regulation, a pure food and drug act and the conservation of the dwindling forests. He negotiated a settlement in the anthracite coal strike

Above: A cartoon from the *New York Herald* 6 February 1905 showing President Theodore Roosevelt in combat with the Railroad Trust. During the Roosevelt administration, 25 indictments of trusts were brought by the Department of Justice. *Far left:* Theodore Roosevelt and his associates in the New York Assembly, 1882. *Left:* Theodore Roosevelt in his army uniform as a lieutenant colonel of the cavalry, 1898. *Right:* Roosevelt wearing buckskins in 1885. This was during the time when he spent part of each year on his ranch in the Dakotas.

Left: The nomination of Theodore Roosevelt for president in 1904. The drawing was captioned 'Scene of Tumultuous Enthusiasm at the First Mention of the President's Name in the Brilliant Nominating Speech at the National Convention at Chicago.' *Right:* Roosevelt and his Cabinet on horseback 10 November 1906. Ever the athlete, Roosevelt at times forced guests to exert themselves physically. *Far right:* T R with Edith, 1903. The children from left to right: Quentin (5), Ted (15), Archie (9), Alice (19), Kermit (13) and Ethel (11). *Below:* A typical 'fire and brimstone' speech.

and told the owners that, if they did not consent to arbitration, he would have the government take and run the mines. He enforced anti-trust legislation and condemned 'malefactors of great wealth.'

In foreign affairs he was equally active. He negotiated a peace settlement which ended the Russo-Japanese War (The Treaty of Portsmouth), for which he received the Nobel Peace Prize. He sent the main American fleet on an expedition around the world and urged the building of an even greater navy. He took part in a conference of the Powers over the African claims of France and Germany. But he is best known for the Panama Canal affair.

The French had attempted to build a canal across Panama. The work had proceeded slowly and the contract with the Republic of Colombia, owner of the canal strip, threatened to expire. Some congressmen were in favor of a rival route in Nicaragua. Suddenly the people of Panama rose in revolt and declared themselves independent of Columbia. Roosevelt at once recognized Panama and threatened to use force if Colombia intervened. He bought the right of way from Panama, not Colombia, and thus left Colombia with a grievance for which, in Harding's time, the United States had to pay solace money. Roosevelt's position was characteristic: 'I took Panama, and while the debate goes on, the canal does, too!'

This was typical of Roosevelt's methods. He quoted an African proverb, 'Walk softly, but carry a big stick!' Sometimes the stick was more in evidence than the soft step.

Since Bryan had been twice defeated the Democrats turned to a conservative and nominated Judge Parker of New York, a little-known and not very impressive politician. Roosevelt in 1904 was re-elected by the biggest popular vote ever given to a nominee up to that time. Only the Solid South held out against him.

In 1908 the Democrats went back to Bryan. Roosevelt would have liked to run again but he had promised in 1904 not to do so. So he supported the candidacy of William Howard Taft, the former able governor of the Philippines and Secretary of War in Roosevelt's cabinet. In later years Taft became Chief Justice of the Supreme Court. In order not to embarrass his successor, Roosevelt went hunting in Africa. He little knew that on his return he would break with his friend and head a new and radical third party.

No Republican since Lincoln has left such an impression on American life as did Roosevelt. His opponents accused him of vanity and egotism but his chief defect was that he was so intense a partisan that he saw everything in black and white. His adverse judgments of the Democratic dead such as Jefferson, and of the living Democrats such as Wilson, were so extreme as to be almost absurd. Nevertheless, although he lacked subtlety, he was so courageous, honest and forthright that few men in political life have been more loved and admired.

THE CRUSADE FOR SOCIAL JUSTICE

Jackson was the symbol and, to a great extent, the leader of the agrarian democracy of the early 19th century, but he was not its sole cause and creator. Similarly, Theodore Roosevelt led the new crusades of the early 20th century, but the cause lay deeper than any one man. Just as the democratic movement of that earlier day reflected the pioneer spirit of the frontier, so the new reform movement reflected the readjustments of American society to an age of industrialism.

This was not, like the anti-slavery crusade, a single issue question. Many things were involved. There were agitations for sundry political reforms, such as women's suffrage, popular election of senators, direct nominating primaries; but the major problems were economic. We have considered the farmers' revolt against the power of the railways and the great corporations, but there was an urban radicalism, too.

On the whole, American labor held a favorable position or fewer immigrants would have poured into the country from less favored lands. But in times of depression thousands were left without employment and wages were severely cut. Capitalism in theory meant free bargaining between employer and employed; but when it came down to actual practice, the big corporation could do without one more workman more easily than the workman could do without a job. Their only security lay in combination, but unionism then involved only a minority of the trades.

A striking example of class antagonism was the Haymarket riot of 1886. Some anarchists were making violent speeches in Chicago, and the police ordered them to disperse. A bomb was thrown, killing seven policemen. Several anarchist agitators were hanged or imprisoned, but in 1893 John Altgeld, a reform governor of Illinois, pardoned the survivors on the grounds that there had been no proven connection between the anarchist orators and the bomb throwing.

Attention Workingmen!

GREAT

MASS-MEETING

TO-NIGHT, at 7.30 o'clock,

AT THE

HAYMARKET, Randolph St., Bet. Desplaines and Halsted.

Good Speakers will be present to denounce the latest atrocious act of the police, the shooting of our fellow-workmen yesterday afternoon.

Workingmen Arm Yourselves and Appear in Full Force!

THE EXECUTIVE COMMITTEE

Achtung, Arbeiter!

Große

Massen-Versammlung

Heute Abend, ½8 Uhr, auf dem

Heumarkt, Randolph-Straße, zwischen Desplaines- u. Halsted-Str.

☞ Gute Redner werden den neuesten Schurkenstreich der Polizei, indem sie gestern Nachmittag unsere Brüder erschoß, geißeln,

☞ Arbeiter, bewaffnet Euch und erscheint massenhaft!

Das Executiv-Comite.

Far left: On 17 July 1877, during the railroad strike on the Baltimore and Ohio Line, some strikers went so far as to drag firemen and engineers from a freight train at Martinsburg, West Virginia. *Left:* An anarchist handbill announcing a mass meeting to be held at Haymarket Square in Chicago 4 May 1886. When the meeting at Haymarket Square began, a bomb was thrown at the police. Fighting followed, and the 'Haymarket Riot' ended with seven policemen dead and 60 wounded; of the strikers, four were dead and 50 wounded. *Far left below:* New York workingmen on strike 10 June 1872. *Below:* The Haymarket Riot.

Left: Coxey's Army in 1894. 'General' Jacob S Coxey of Massillon, Ohio had advocated that Congress issue $4500 million in legal tender notes to be spent on building good roads, and wages of $1.50 per day would be paid to the workers who needed employment on these roads. He also recommended non-interest-bearing bonds be floated to pay for the construction of schools, paved streets and courthouses. To promote his ideas Coxey organized a march of the unemployed on Washington. The march started on Easter Sunday 1894 and on 1 May 500 men arrived in the Capital, where they were arrested. *Above:* United States troops protecting a train during the Pullman Strike of 1894.

Altgeld again appeared in the limelight when, in 1894, there was a strike at the Pullman Car Works. President Cleveland enjoined the strike, arguing that the Constitution gave the federal government jurisdiction over interstate commerce. Altgeld protested in the name of the state rights of Illinois. Eugene Debs, the leader of the strikers, became a Socialist and was for many years the presidential candidate of the small Socialist Party.

The most effective labor organization was the American Federation of Labor, organized by Samuel Gompers. Later in the century a rival organization, the Congress of Industrial Organizations (CIO) was founded, and the two eventually merged. The railroad brotherhoods, the merchant seamen and the miners had their own organizations.

In the meantime there was a parallel 'literature of exposure' (sometimes called the 'muckrakers,' from a casual allusion by President Roosevelt to Bunyan's 'Man with the Muckrake') directed against political dishonesty and corporate greed. Among the group were Lincoln Steffens, Ida Tarbell, Ray Stannard Baker, William Allen White and the Socialist Upton Sinclair.

The women's suffrage agitation was first launched in New York State in 1848, but the initial victory came in 1869 when the Territory of Wyoming adopted equal suffrage for all elections. This was reaffirmed in 1890 when Wyoming became a state, and by the end of the century some Rocky Mountain states had full women's suffrage and several other states had a limited suffrage for certain offices, such as school elections.

The movement progressed slowly in the East, and not at all in the South, until the First World War, although Anna Howard Shaw and Carrie Chapman Catt furnished able leadership. At the end of the war, it became national law through the 19th amendment to the Constitution. There was nothing in the United States comparable to the violent tactics of the militant English 'suffragettes.'

The direct primaries issue needs a word of explanation. Originally the national party conventions were the top of a hierarchy: first the local caucus attended by all party members who took the trouble to come, then the county and state conventions. Since there was pressure at every stage from professional politicians, the voters in November were really offered only a choice between candidates nominated by the Republican and Democratic political machines. Now it became the rule for the voters to choose members of the conventions directly, and sometimes to instruct them on which presidential aspirant to vote for.

By the 16th and 17th amendments Congress was authorized to levy a federal income tax, and the people at large (not, as hitherto, the state legislatures) to choose senators. There were local movements to adopt the Swiss devices of the initiative, referendum and recall, and for proportional representation, but these had no success except in a few western localities.

Left: Samuel Gompers in a photograph taken in 1904. In 1881 Gompers was one of the founders of the American Federation of Labor, and with the exception of one year, served as its president from 1885 until his death in 1924. He has been called the man responsible for the eight hour day and the setting up of the Federal Department of Commerce and Labor in 1903. *Above:* The first Women's Rights meeting, which laid the foundation for Woman Suffrage, was held under the leadership of Elizabeth Cady Stanton in Seneca Falls, New York 20 June 1848. *Top far right:* In 1888 leaders of the suffrage movement met to plan the international suffrage meeting. Susan B Anthony is second from the left in the first row, and Elizabeth Cady Stanton is third from right in the first row. *Below far left:* Lincoln Steffens, the American journalist and editor. *Below center:* Upton Sinclair, the revolutionary writer. *Below:* William Allen White, the editor. *Right:* Suffragettes in Asbury Park, New Jersey.

THE REPUBLICAN SPLIT OF 1912

Liberal Republicans were disappointed by the administration of William Howard Taft. They had looked for a second edition of Roosevelt, for had not Taft been in his cabinet and hadn't he been warmly supported by Roosevelt for the presidency? But Taft proved to be a conservative in opinion and easy-going by temperament. He appointed conservatives to office and relied on the advice of party regulars in Congress.

Moreover, the Republicans had two specific quarrels with Taft. He had signed the Payne-Aldrich tariff, which raised as many duties as it diminished, and he had sided with Secretary of the Interior Ballinger against the ardent conservationist Gifford Pinchot, a friend of Roosevelt's

So they looked for an alternative. Some were inclined to favor Robert La Follette of Wisconsin, a more consistent radical even than Roosevelt. But it became plain that he could not defeat Taft for renomination. They finally persuaded Roosevelt to enter the race. Roosevelt took several primaries but was defeated by states which chose delegates in convention.

Roosevelt denounced the seating of Taft delegates against those chosen by the Roosevelt faction, and proclaimed an independent candidacy. The new party was called the National Progressive Party, but was popularly nicknamed the 'Bull Moose Party' from a phrase of Roosevelt's ('I feel as strong as a Bull Moose.').

In the meantime the Democrats were having a contest of their own. The preferred candidate, who at one period had a majority, though not the required two-thirds, of the delegates, was Champ Clark of Missouri, speaker of the House of Representatives. The runner-up was Woodrow

Opposite top: A cartoon of Theodore Roosevelt and William Howard Taft entitled 'Goodness Gracious, I Must Have Been Dozing.' Roosevelt watches from outside the window as 'Mother' Taft has trouble with her knitting. The animals causing the trouble are labeled 'The House,' 'The Senate,' 'The Courts' and 'The Cabinet.' *Left:* William Howard Taft, the twenty-seventh president of the United States. *Above:* President Taft, although a huge man of some 350 pounds, did get some exercise. He is shown playing golf 28 June 1909.

Wilson, governor of New Jersey and former president of Princeton University. There was also the usual crop of favorite sons.

Bryan, who had been three times the defeated candidate of the Democrats, resolved that if he could not be 'king', at least he would be 'king-maker.' When Tammany Hall shifted its support to Champ Clark, Bryan shifted his to Wilson, and eventually Wilson was nominated, with Thomas Marshall of Indiana for vice president.

There was now a three-cornered election and it was the only occasion in American history when an ex-president, a current president and a future president all competed. During the campaign an anti-third term fanatic shot and wounded Roosevelt while he was addressing a group of voters, who nevertheless insisted on continuing his speech. As is often the case, the attempted assassination boomeranged and added to the Roosevelt vote.

Nevertheless, Wilson was an easy victor. The Republican split had done for the Democrats what the Democrat split of 1860 had done for the Republicans. Roosevelt and his new party came in second and Taft carried only Utah and Vermont.

Liberalism seemed at high tide. Roosevelt's 'new nationalism' and Wilson's 'new freedom' both championed radical reforms, and the Socialist candidate, Eugene Debs, increased his popular vote. But the First World War turned attention from domestic to foreign issues and the decade of the 1920s was eminently conservative.

WOODROW WILSON AND HIS TIMES

President Wilson was something new in American politics. He was not the first scholarly president – some had taught school and many had written books – but he was the first professional educator to hold that post. Only a brief term as governor of New Jersey separated his purely academic career from the presidency. There had been some who had thought of him as a safe and sane alternative to the persistent Bryan, but by 1912 he was classed as a liberal.

With strong support in Congress Wilson was able to carry out most of his contemplated domestic reforms with little difficulty. The tariff was lowered, the national banking system organized and the eight hour day established for the railroads. Favorable legislation improved the position of the trade unions.

His chief problems arose in foreign affairs. As a gesture of gratitude he made Bryan his secretary of state, but he kept foreign policy in his own hands. As the British would say, he was his own foreign minister.

As so often before, the Mexican volcano was in eruption. General Porfiro Diaz, whose strong hand held popular discontent in check for many years, had passed from the scene, and his liberal successor, Francisco Madero, was unable to prevent a reactionary *coup d'état* by General Victoriano Huerta. Most foreign governments recognized Huerta, but Wilson refused to do so. He encouraged the Constitutionalists under Venustiano Carranza and twice he intervened directly, on one occasion occupying the port of Vera Cruz, on another letting General John Pershing pursue Pancho Villa's raiders across the border. These raiders had attacked American towns in the Southwest. But, not wishing a second Mexican War, he had withdrawn the American forces in a short space of time.

Below: Gen John J Pershing in Mexico. Francisco 'Pancho' Villa, a Mexican revolutionary, twice crossed the American border in 1916, raiding towns and murdering Americans. *Bottom:* The inauguration of Woodrow Wilson in 1913. *Right:* Woodrow Wilson, the twenty-eighth US president.

All Wilson's other difficulties, whether foreign or domestic, vanished into insignificance when the war broke out in Europe in 1914 and he is remembered today chiefly by his policies during the war and the subsequent peace conference.

Although both Roosevelt and Wilson were often classed together as liberal reformers, there was no personal empathy between them. Roosevelt regarded Wilson as an ineffectual academic, all words without deeds, and Wilson considered Roosevelt a political Peter Pan who had never really grown up.

Roosevelt was in doubt about continuing the new party which he had founded. It had given him a heavy personal vote in 1912, but it had elected few members of Congress or state officials. With the coming of the European War he thought it best to close the Republican ranks and defeat Wilson. So he accepted, though without much enthusiasm, the Republican nomination of Charles Evans Hughes, a member of the Supreme Court and a former reform governor of New York.

The election of 1916 was very close, in fact the result was finally determined by belated returns from California. Wilson's second term was entirely filled by issues arising from World War I.

Left: A Wilson campaign poster of 1916 displayed in St Louis. The poster lauds him for giving 'peace with honor' and credits him with giving the United States 'Our First Real Preparedness to Insure Continuance of Peace.' *Top:* William Jennings Bryan was Wilson's Secretary of State from 5 March 1913 to 8 June 1915. *Above:* A cartoon of Kaiser Wilhelm II after the sinking of the *Sussex* by a submarine 24 March 1916. *Opposite:* Another warmongering cartoon protesting the loss of American lives in the submarine attacks on British vessels.

WAR IN EUROPE

Ever since the Franco-Prussian War of 1870–71 Europe had been substantially at peace. Wars were fought but in out-of-the-way places, such as Manchuria, South Africa or the half-Asiatic Balkans. The peace, however, was precarious. The six great powers of Europe, Britain, France, Russia, Germany, Austria-Hungary and Italy, were constantly increasing their armaments on land and sea and, later, in the air. On several occasions diplomatic disputes threatened war, but were smoothed over by last minute compromises. In the 1880s Otto von Bismarck had bound Germany, Austria and Italy into a triple alliance. France and Russia formed a counter-alliance in the 1890s.

Great Britain continued to the end of the 19th century in her 'splendid isolation', but sought friends in the new century – a limited alliance with Japan in 1902 and *ententes* (diplomatic agreements) with France in 1904 and Russia in 1907.

In 1914 a Serb fanatic in Bosnia killed the heir to the Austrian throne. The Austrian government resolved to punish Serbia for her anti-Austrian intrigues and demand an unlimited submission in a formidable ultimatum. Russia, fearing to lose her own influence in the Balkans, protested and demanded a peaceful solution. Germany had already given private assurances of support to Austria but, alarmed by Russian intervention, sought to modify Austria's intransigence. It was too late. Austria attacked Serbia, Russia mobilized her army, Germany threatened Russia and on 1 August made war on Russia and on Russia's ally, France.

— Les lois ! je les fais moi-même. Je sais donc ce qu'elles valent.   (*Boston Record*, de Boston.)

In order to win a quick victory, Germany struck at France along the flat plains of Belgium, although international agreements had made Belgium 'perpetually neutral'.

This determined the action of Great Britain, and on 4 August the British government declared war on Germany. This was not only a fulfillment of British treaty obligations, but also a matter of self-defense. For centuries it had been a principle of British foreign policy not to let the Low Countries (Holland, Belgium, Luxembourg) fall into the hands of any ambitious great power on the continent. On this issue they had fought Spain under Philip II and France under Louis XIV and Napoleon.

Other nations soon joined the fray. Turkey and Bulgaria entered on the German side; Montenegro, Rumania and, later, Greece on the anti-German side, the so-called 'Triple Entente' group. Italy had been a reluctant partner of her old foe Austria but now took the other side in the hope of getting some Italian-speaking districts from Austria-Hungary. Japan seized a Chinese port from Germany.

Had the war been as brief as both sides expected, the United States would not have been involved. But it settled down to a slow war of attrition between entrenchments extending from the Alps to the sea. In the west, Germany had occupied Belgium and a corner of France. In the east, she had forced Russia out of Austrian and Russian Poland. But still there was no decision.

FRANK HOLLAND, in Reynolds's Newspap

Knocked into a Cocked Hat

Opposite top: Prince Otto von Bismarck, the mastermind of European peace, surrounded by family and friends. Had his diplomatic policies not been subverted, World War I might not have happened. *Left:* An American World War I cartoon showing Kaiser Wilhelm II making up his own laws, saying: 'The laws! They are made by me. This is why I know their value.' *Top:* Emperor Franz Joseph of the Austro-Hungarian Empire. *Above:* A World War I cartoon showing the Allies descending on the Kaiser. *Right:* An American cartoon of 15 May 1915 in which the Kaiser is pondering his response to the American note. Humanity stands behind him, waiting for his answer.

QU'EST-CE QUE VA ÊTRE SA RÉPONSE ?

Composition de CESARE. (*The Sun*, journal quotidien de New-York, 15 Mai 1915.)

* Le Kaiser méditant sa réponse à la note américaine. C'est en vain que l'Humanité se tient à ses côtés, inquiète et anxieuse.

AMERICA ENTERS THE WAR

When President Wilson proclaimed neutrality it was taken as a matter of course. It is true that in America sympathy was unequally divided; a majority of the public sympathized with Britain and France and, above all, with Belgium. But they had cheered from the sidelines before without becoming involved in the game. Traditions of neutrality were strong. The United States had never had a peacetime alliance, its only wars with European powers (two with Britain, one with Spain) had been fought on the high seas or on the American continent. American volunteers had sometimes entered foreign conflicts, but never in American uniforms.

The first doubts that the United States could maintain neutrality came with the German submarine campaign against merchant shipping. The British fleet commanded the seas; the only effective way the Germans could strike back was by unexpected attack on unprotected merchant ships. For this purpose the submarine, shrouded by the waters from lurking cruisers and destroyers, was the most effective weapon.

In 1915 the great British liner *Lusitania* was sunk and more than a hundred Americans were drowned. President Wilson made a vigorous protest. Bryan resigned as secretary of state, fearing that the United States was drifting toward war. Ex-president Roosevelt demanded action. He accused Wilson of using 'weasel words' and being a 'Byzantine logothete', which sent most people to their dictionaries.

Wilson still tried to avoid war, hoping perhaps to negotiate a peaceful settlement when both sides were tired of fighting, as Roosevelt had done with the Russo-Japanese conflict. But sinkings still continued. In the campaign of 1916 most politicians ignored the question of intervention and talked instead about Mexico and the railroad strike. The Republicans, except for Roosevelt, took no definite stand, fearing perhaps to lose either the German-American vote or the 'preparedness' supporters. Many Democrats praised Wilson for 'keeping us out of war.'

Once assured of his re-election, Wilson asked both European sides to state their aims. The Entente Allies prepared a statement; the Germans

Les pirates décernant au Kaiser la couronne qu'il a bien méritée.

VOTE FOR
WILSON
AND
MARSHALL
SEABURY
AND
McCOMBS
WOMEN'S BUREAU
DEMOCRATIC NATIONAL COMMITTEE

FOR
PRESIDENT
WOODROW
WILSON

WHO BROKE THE
MONEY TRUST?

WHO KEEPS US
OUT OF WAR?

WHO STANDS FOR
THE 8 HOUR DAY?

WHO EXTENDED
THE PARCEL POST?

WHO GAVE THE FARMER
RURAL CREDITS?

VOTE FOR WILSON
PEACE WITH HONOR
PROSPERITY
PREPAREDNESS

Above left: A French journal reprint of an American cartoon of World War I published in the *New York Telegram* in May 1915. The Kaiser is being crowned by three infamous pirates. *Below left:* A cartoon by John T McCutcheon that appeared in the *Chicago Tribune* in 1915. For decades the *Tribune* was the

oustanding isolationist paper in the United States. Here, the American people are declaring, in unison, their desire to remain isolated from Europe. *Above:* Wilson's campaign for reelection was based on his promise to keep America out of World War I.

did not, but they offered to enter into secret negotiations. When the Germans announced their intention to renew unrestricted submarine warfare, Wilson broke diplomatic relations with them and proposed 'armed neutrality,' merchant ships to carry defensive artillery.

There were other causes for conflict. For example, by the 'Zimmermann note,' the Germans offered Mexico Texas, New Mexico and Arizona in case the United States declared war on Germany. There were sabotage plots against American munition plants.

Finally, in April, 1917 Wilson asked Congress for a declaration of war: 'The world must be made safe for democracy. Its peace must be planted upon the tested foundations of political liberty.'

The declaration of war carried, but not without some opposition. Six negative votes were cast in the Senate and 50 in the House of Representatives.

"All the News That's Fit to Print."

The New York Times.

EXTRA
5:30 A. M.

VOL. LXIV...NO. 20,923. .....   NEW YORK, SATURDAY, MAY 8, 1915.—TWENTY-FOUR PAGES.   ONE CENT

LUSITANIA SUNK BY A SUBMARINE, PROBABLY 1,260 DEAD;
TWICE TORPEDOED OFF IRISH COAST; SINKS IN 15 MINUTES;
CAPT. TURNER SAVED, FROHMAN AND VANDERBILT MISSING;
WASHINGTON BELIEVES THAT A GRAVE CRISIS IS AT HAND

SHOCKS THE PRESIDENT

Washington Deeply Stirred by the Loss of American Lives.

BULLETINS AT WHITE HOUSE

Wilson Reads Them Closely, but Is Silent on the Nation's Course.

HINTS OF CONGRESS CALL

Loss of Lusitania Recalls Firm Tone of Our First Warning to Germany.

CAPITAL FULL OF RUMORS

Reports That Liner Was to be Sunk Were Heard Before Actual News Came.

Special to The New York Times.

WASHINGTON, May 7.— Never since that April day, three years ago, when word came that the Titanic had gone down, has Washington been so stirred as it is tonight over the sinking of the Lusitania. The early reports told that there had been no loss of life, but the relief that there advices caused gave way to the greatest concern late the evening when it became known that there had been many deaths. Although they are profoundly reticent, officials realize that this tragedy, involving the loss of American citizens, is likely to bring about a crisis in the international relations of the United States.

It is pointed out that the sinking of the Lusitania is the outcome of a series of incidents that have been the cause of concern to this Government in its endeavor to maintain a strictly neutral position in the great European war.

Nation's Course in Doubt.

It is impossible to say tonight what effect the loss of American lives on the Lusitania will have on the Government. Judged from the little that can be learned it is a safe prediction that President Wilson will continue

The Lost Cunard Steamship Lusitania

SOME DEAD TAKEN ASHORE

Several Hundred Survivors at Queenstown and Kinsale.

STEWARD TELLS OF DISASTER

(partially obscured by advertisement clipping)

ADVERTISEMENT.

NOTICE!

TRAVELLERS intending to embark on the Atlantic voyage are reminded that a state of war exists between Germany and her allies and Great Britain and her allies; that the zone of war includes the waters adjacent to the British Isles; that, in accordance with formal notice given by the Imperial German Government, vessels flying the flag of Great Britain, or of any of her allies, are liable to destruction in those waters and that travellers sailing in the war zone on ships of Great Britain or her allies do so at their own risk.

IMPERIAL GERMAN EMBASSY
WASHINGTON, D. C., APRIL 22, 1915.

Cunard Office Here Besieged for News; Fate of 1,918 on Lusitania Long in Doubt

Nothing Heard from the Well-Known Passengers on Board—Story of Disaster Long Unconfirmed While Anxious Crowds Seek Details.

Official news of the sinking of the Lusitania yesterday reached New York in fragmentary reports, and several hours elapsed between the first unverified rumor of the disaster and the cable messages that told at night of the saving of some of the passengers and gave meagre details of the most sensational incident of its kind in the war.

The early messages that indicated all on board had been saved reassured

List of Saved Includes Capt. Turner; Vanderbilt and Frohman Reported Lost

LONDON, Saturday, May 8, 5:50 A. M. The Press Bureau has received from the British Admiralty at Queenstown a report that all the torpedo boats and tugs and armed trawlers, except the Heron, which went out from Queenstown to the relief of the Lusitania have returned.

Saw the Submarine 100 Ya... and Watched Torpedo as...

Ernest Cowper, a Toronto Newspaper... Attack, Seen from Ship's Rai... Used in Torpedoes, Say Othe...

Queenstown, Saturday,
May 8, 3:18 A. M.
A sharp lookout for submarines was kept aboard the Lusitania as she approached the Irish coast, according to Ernest Cowper, a Toronto newspaper man, who was

LONDON, Saturday,
The Cunard liner Lusitania, which sailed out of New York

Opposite top: *The New York Times* and most of the other daily papers in the United States headlined the sinking of the *Lusitania* in their issues of 8 May 1915. The ship had been torpedoed the day before. *Opposite bottom:* The *Lusitania* embarking on a voyage. *Right:* An artist superimposed the crosshairs of a German submarine's periscope on a photograph of the *Lusitania. Below:* Wilson called Congress into special session 2 April 1917 and delivered his war message, coining the phrase, 'The world must be made safe for Democracy.'

THE FIRST WORLD WAR

Opposite: A solitary soldier guards a shipyard on the East Coast, 1917. *Below:* Col Edward M House of Texas was an intimate advisor of President Wilson: a photograph of the two men at Roslyn, Long Island, New York. *Bottom:* American troops in France cooking breakfast after a night march in the rain.

The United States, once it decided on war, determined to send an army to Europe. It would have been possible to have made it a naval war with some token volunteers to be sent to Europe, but, instead, conscription was adopted, a device never used before except in the Civil War. At that time there had been complaints, both North and South, that the wealthy could escape the draft. But now the wealthy playboy stood less chance of being passed over than the shipwright or expert munitions worker who were needed on the home front.

At sea America sent aid to Europe under convoy and helped hunt down submarines. An expeditionary force under General John Pershing was organized and officers trained in special camps. Herbert Hoover, who had superintended Belgian Relief, took over the rationing of food, and America had 'meatless' and 'wheatless' days. Huge loans were granted to European belligerents.

American intervention came at a dark hour. Russia had collapsed in revolution and there were mutinies in France and Italy. Without aid from the United States the war might have lasted until a state of mutual exhaustion occurred instead of coming to a definite conclusion. In all, the United States trained about 4 million men and sent 2 million into the war zones. The United States had over 50 thousand battle deaths and more than that were killed by the influenza epidemic of 1918.

President Wilson wisely did not interfere with the strategy of the war, but his diplomatic contributions were most significant. He made the most specific offer of peace terms coming from any nation – the so-called 'Fourteen Points.'

Five of these were general; 'open covenants of peace,' the freedom of the seas, removal of economic barriers, reduction of armaments and 'a general association of nations' for guaranteeing the independence and integrity of all nations.

The other nine were territorial: a fair readjustment of colonial claims, Alsace-Lorraine to be given to France, self-government for minorities in Turkey and Austria-Hungary, evacuation of Belgium and Russia, a reconstituted Poland with 'access to the sea.'

By 1918 the position of the Central Powers had become desperate. Austria-Hungary, Bulgaria and Turkey had ceased to be effective allies and Germany was fighting practically alone against increasing odds. Finally she asked for an armistice on the basis of Wilson's points. With two modifications the European allies agreed: the question of 'freedom of the seas' was to be left for later discussion and the 'restoration' of invaded territory was to include their reconstruction and indemnification for damage done.

A wave of revolution swept over Europe. The Russian tsardom had collapsed in 1917 and later in the year a Communist dictatorship had taken over. In 1918 the German Kaiser Wilhelm fled to neutral Holland and Austria-Hungary was splintered into half a dozen national states. When the Peace Conference of 1919 met in Paris, the three great empires of eastern Europe – Russia, Austria-Hungary and Turkey – had already broken into pieces, and the task of the peacemakers was merely to determine in detail the new boundaries.

Below: American soldiers wearing captured German helmets and breastplates. The one at the left is holding a French Chauchat machine gun, the second from the left a service rifle and the one at the right an antitank rifle. *Right:* Troops of the 64th Infantry Brigade, 32nd Division advancing while in support of the first line near Romagne-sous-Montfaucon. Meuse 18 October 1918. *Below right:* Two American soldiers in a shell crater with their heavy machine gun in the Meuse-Argonne, France.

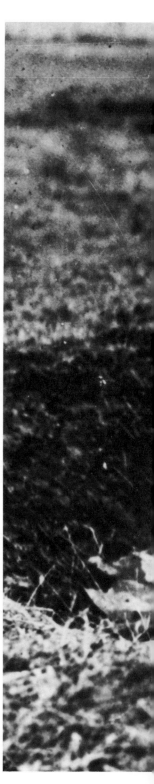

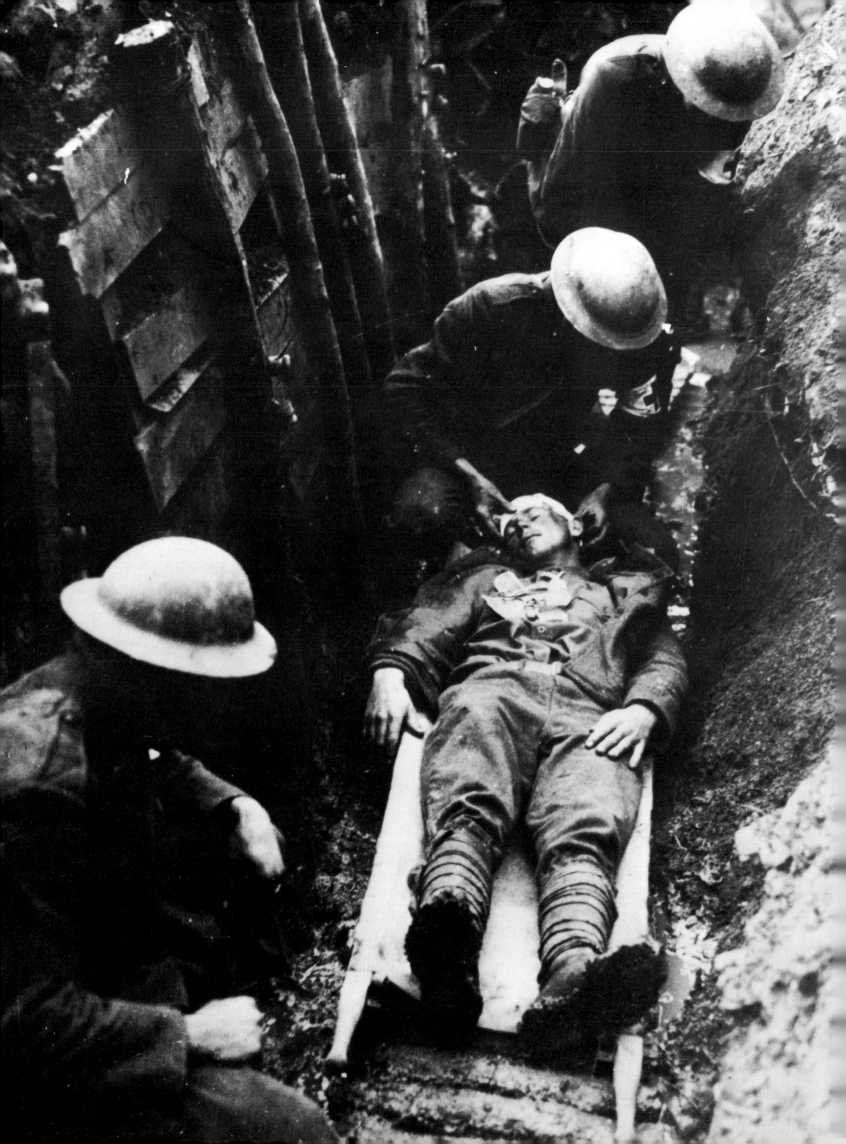

Opposite: An American marine receiving first aid before being sent to a military hospital at the rear of the trenches 22 March 1918. *Above:* United States Army troops cheering the Armistice 11 November 1918. *Right:* United States officials of the Peace Conference at the Hotel Crillon in Paris 18 December 1918. Left to right: Col Edward M House, Robert Lansing, Woodrow Wilson, Henry White and Gen Tasker Bliss.

PART 4
THE NEW DAY, SINCE 1919

World War I, which was to President Wilson a great crusade, was to many of his countrymen a necessary, but temporary, interruption. The country became isolationistic, rejecting the Treaty of Versailles, the League of Nations Covenant and even the World Court. The tariff was raised and, for the first time, a numerical limit was imposed on immigration. Three conservative Republican presidents, in ascending order of ability Warren G Harding, Calvin Coolidge and Herbert Hoover, ruled the decade of the 1920s.

But in 1929 prosperity turned into a depression and Franklin Roosevelt, in the 1930s, inaugurated a 'New Deal' of measures designed to stabilize the economy and find work for the unemployed. He was elected to four terms. His first two terms were eras of domestic reform, but his third term was in the time of World War II, and, in his fourth term he died and was succeeded by Harry S Truman. General Dwight Eisenhower was then twice elected as a Republican, but the Democrats came back into power with John Kennedy, assassinated in mid-term, and Lyndon Johnson of Texas.

Relations with Soviet Russia, America's ally in World War II, became strained and the resulting 'Cold War' was punctuated by two anti-Communist campaigns in Korea and Vietnam.

Richard Nixon was twice elected, but resigned in his second term, which was completed by Gerald Ford. Jimmy Carter, another Democrat and southerner, followed, and then a Republican, Ronald Reagan of California, was elected to two successive terms.

The second centennial in 1976 found the United States still governed by the stable, popular Constitution of 1787. Had the founding fathers returned, they would probably have considered that their daring experiment of 1776 had been crowned with success.

A US Army tank advances through the shattered remains of a German convoy, France, 1944.

THE REACTION TO ISOLATION

President Wilson was determined to go to Paris in person to take part in the making of the peace treaties. He was criticized for this, but he had to deal with the responsible leaders of Britain, France and other Great Powers, and he felt that he could negotiate more freely at first hand. More dubious was his failure to make any leading Republican a member of his negotiating team. The Republicans therefore felt that he was running peacemaking too much as a one-man show.

There were two things that he particularly had in mind: a strong League of Nations to diminish the risk of future wars, and 'self-determination' in fixing the new frontiers according to the wishes of their local population. As with most peace settlements after a general war, the treaties represented a series of compromises. The French felt that not enough had been done to assure that Germany would be harmless in the future. There were pacifists who felt that too many concessions had been made to French intransigence. Russia, then in the throes of civil war, was not consulted at all. Many people in the United States wanted to get back quickly to 'business as usual' instead of worrying about Macedonia and Mesopotamia.

When Wilson returned to the United States, a group of senators, led by Henry Cabot Lodge of Massachusetts, decided to attack the Covenant of the League of Nations by 'reservations' which would free the United States from any obligation to defend foreign countries. Wilson said that this would 'cut the heart from the League' and refused compromise. He

Left: Badly weakened by his fight for the League of Nations in Paris, Wilson returned to Washington, where he suffered a paralytic stroke. When he did recover, he lacked physical vigor. *Opposite below:* A picture taken 11 November 1918 showing crowds in front of the Chamber of Deputies in Paris awaiting the official announcement of the armistice. *Below:* Senator Henry Cabot Lodge was opposed to the League of Nations and was the leader of the Republican Party's shift to isolationism. *Right:* The signing of the World War I Peace Treaty at Versailles.

made a series of speeches for the League, but was immobilized by a paralytic stroke in the midst of his campaign. Congress was already controlled by the Republicans, and in 1920 they nominated Senator Warren G Harding and the Democrats James Cox, both newspaper publishers from Ohio. The Republican victory was overwhelming.

The Harding administration made a separate peace with the Central Powers and ignored altogether the peace treaties and the League of Nations. There was a strong reaction against the war. But there is a distinction to be made here. It was not a reaction to pacifism, or Robert La Follette, the leader of the opposition to the war, would have done better when he ran for president on a third party ticket in 1924. Only a minority felt that the United States could, or should, have avoided entering the war, but there was an annoyed feeling that the war should have stayed away from America and confined itself to Europe where it belonged. It was the only war which produced no presidential candidates trading on their military prestige.

Something was done for peace, however. In Harding's time, with the able assistance of Charles Evans Hughes as secretary of state, there was signed a naval limitation agreement affecting the American, British, Japanese, French and Italian navies (those of Germany and Russia had been temporarily eliminated by the war). But, in general, the United States retired within itself.

Isolation showed itself in other ways. A high protective tariff was adopted and numerical restrictions imposed on foreign immigration. These laws established a quota, fixing the number of immigrants from any country at a percentage of those of that nationality already domiciled in the United States. This was done deliberately to favor the 'older' immigration from northwest Europe against the 'newer' from southern and eastern Europe.

Another symptom of national isolationism was the revival of the Ku Klux Klan, directed primarily against the Blacks, as the reconstruction Klan had been, but even more against the Roman Catholics like the old Know Nothing Party of the 1850s. On the issue of opposing the Klan, the Democratic convention of 1924 was deadlocked for three weeks and 103 ballots between William Gibbs McAdoo, Wilson's son-in-law, who wished to ignore the question, and the Catholic Alfred E Smith, the governor of New York.

The great failure of the Harding administration, like Grant's, was in the appointment of unfit men to office. Secretary of the Interior Albert B Fall went to prison for his part in selling government oil wells (Elk Hills and Teapot Dome) to private interests in return for a personal 'loan'. Attorney-General Harry Daugherty resigned under fire. Colonel Charles Forbes of the Veterans Bureau was convicted of graft.

Harding died in the middle of his first term and was succeeded by Vice President Calvin Coolidge, who easily won, running against John W Davis, the Democrat, and Robert La Follette, the Progressive, in the election of 1928. Coolidge was a taciturn Yankee from Massachusetts. He initiated few changes and resisted the farmers' clamor for price supports. He accepted the Kellogg-Briand peace agreement which, in general terms, repudiated war but provided no machinery to enforce peace.

Above: Calvin Coolidge, the thirtieth president of the United States, with his wife Grace. He had been Harding's vice-president, succeeding him on his death 2 August 1923. *Below:* President Warren G Harding throwing out the first ball of the baseball season, Washington D C 12 April 1922. *Right:* During the 1920s, the Ku Klux Klan became popular again. This parade was staged in Washington.

JUGGERNAUT.

Left: After the Harding administration many scandals came to light, some of them involving oil company kickbacks. It is probable that Harding never knew the whole truth about these scandals, but he knew enough in 1923 to make him sick at heart, and this may have had something to do with his collapse and death.
Above: Albert B Fall who had been Harding's Secretary of the Interior, the villain of the Teapot Dome Scandal, shown at the left, arriving at the District of Columbia Supreme Court on the charge of bribery concerning the Elk Hills naval oil reserve leasing.
Right: A photograph of the Senate Investigating Committee during the hearings on the Teapot Dome Scandal 24 March 1924.

PROHIBITION AND CRIME

There had been a Prohibition Party for many years, vainly nominating candidates every four years, but getting so few votes that it had no influence on the general result of the election. Much more effective was the Anti-Saloon League, which had won over many states in the rural South and West to statewide prohibition.

At the end of World War I the 18th amendment to the Constitution made prohibition nationwide. This was more precisely spelled out by the Volstead Act, which forbade intoxicating drinks with more than one-half of one per cent alcohol.

From the start there were difficulties in the enforcement of the law. Americans have never been distinguished for obedience to laws which they do not like; there was a 'whiskey rebellion' against government revenue agents in Washington's time, and at all times there were 'moonshiners' who distilled illicit liquor, and 'bootleggers' who transported it. With the new, more drastic restrictions, the difficulty became even greater; trucks running at night, or smugglers coming from offshore ships catered to those willing to pay the higher prices. There is a good deal of evidence that alcoholic consumption decreased among the poor. Those who could afford it, however, drank almost as much as ever, but they often consumed poor liquor.

Below: Many rumrunner's boats were stopped by federal authorities. Often they were found to be jam-packed with illegal liquor. *Left:* It also often happened that police apprehended bootleggers and placed the confiscated liquor in government vaults, as they are doing here in Washington DC.

Left: Many people started carrying their own bottles or flasks of whiskey on their persons. The Department of Justice was swamped with arrests and prohibition cases flooded the courts. Thirty-five hundred civil cases and 65,000 criminal cases were brought to court within a period of less than two years. *Below:* Demonstrations were held urging the repeal of prohibition.

The great argument which kept the experiment going during the decade of the 1920s was that abstinence increased prosperity. But this was proved wrong by the 1929 depression, and prohibition was repealed by the 21st amendment.

America has always been a violent country, and the decade showed little increase in crime as a whole, although there was a welcome decrease in lynchings. But there were some troublesome new forms of crime, such as racketeering. A typical example would be a 'machinist's protective association'. Those refusing to join would not only forfeit protection but also be exposed to 'accidents', such as slashed tires.

The kidnapping and murder of Colonel Charles A Lindbergh's infant child led to legislation permitting federal authorities to intervene in such cases if time enough had elapsed to permit the carrying of the kidnapped person across a state line.

Some captains of organized crime, such as Al Capone, and bank robbers, such as John Dillinger, became national figures, more widely known than most political leaders, or, indeed, than anyone except a few athletes and motion picture stars. When the eminent educator, Charles Eliot, former president of Harvard, died almost simultaneously with Rudolph Valentino, the movie actor, some newspapers editorially deplored the fact that the less important man had the wider publicity, and continued to give a page to Valentino for every column about Eliot.

Left: Some criminals became folk heroes. John Dillinger, the bank robber, was such a man. He is shown on friendly terms with the sheriff who put him in jail. *Below:* George 'Machine Gun' Kelly was another folk hero. Here he is being taken to a plane in Memphis to be flown to Oklahoma City to stand trial for a kidnapping. *Right:* Al Capone (wearing hat), the 'King of the Chicago Underworld,' 22 March 1930.

THE GOLDEN DECADE

The period immediately following a great war is usually a troubled one; returning peace brings its own problems and there is not the same patriotic unity which prevailed in wartime. One thinks of the 'critical period' between the Revolution and the ratification of the Constitution; of the reconstruction years following the Civil War. It was not otherwise in the 1920s – to that decade such uncomplimentary names have been given as 'the roaring decade,' the 'era of wonderful nonsense,' and 'the fatuous twenties.'

But there were some bright spots. Although there was a slight recession around 1921, affecting chiefly the farmers, the general scene was prosperous. This was not caused, as some soured foreign critics supposed, by war profiteering, for the war was actually an economic burden, increasing taxes and public debts and dislocating normal commerce. The chief cause was the rapid multiplication of mechanism in industry.

The automobile, largely a sporting vehicle for the wealthy in the early days of the century, became almost ubiquitous. Trucks and buses cut deeply into the profits of the railroads.

New domestic appliances were the rage. Few families were without telephones. Electric refrigerators replaced the ice box, as it, in turn, had replaced the deep cellar. The movie industry, centered in California where clear skies and a varied landscape offered the best environment for photography, became a vast amusement enterprise. Radio brought the outside world into the home.

Below: America had become automobile-crazy. This is a showroom in Washington DC in 1922. *Bottom:* New kinds of electrical appliances were also all the rage. This store in Louisville had at least 16 clerks ready to sell the housewife labor-saving devices. *Right:* It was the day of *The Ziegfeld Follies* on Broadway. Claudia Dell was but one of the hundreds of 'Ziegfeld Girls' who entertained Broadway audiences in the 1920s.

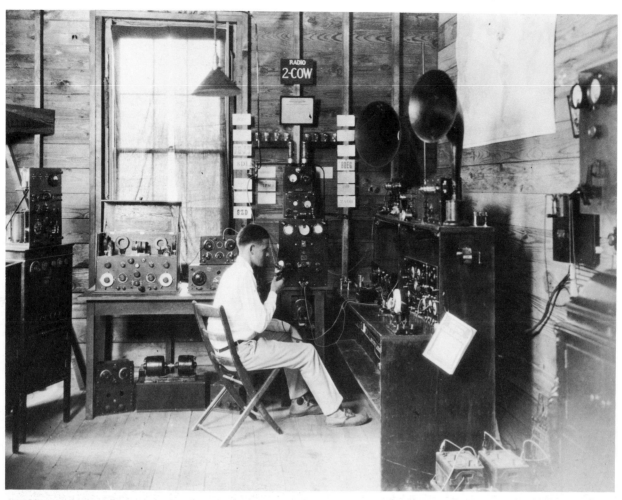

Left: Another new invention that captivated the country was the radio. Hundreds of people set up 'ham' radio stations. The 'Radio Shack' shown was located in New Paltz, New York in 1922. *Below left:* The Flapper Look was in style. These women of the 'Flaming Youth' generation cultivated boyish figures, bobbed their hair, and rolled their silk stockings below the knee. *Below:* The hero of the decade was Charles A Lindbergh (third from right), who made the first solo crossing of the Atlantic in an airplane. He left Roosevelt Field (near Mineola), New York in his Ryan monoplane *The Spirit of St Louis* on 20 May 1927, and reached Le Bourget airfield near Paris 21 May. His flying time was 33½ hours for the 3610 mile trip.

The airplane has never become the major carrier of freight, but its speed made it the favorite for mail and passenger service. When Lindbergh made his solo flight to Paris in 1927 it not only made him a folk hero, but also opened a new era in transportation.

From the earliest times, Americans had moved to new localities where they could work more profitably; now for the first time, millions went south to the sun belt of Florida, California and the mountainous Southwest, where they could play to better advantage.

College and university populations grew rapidly, and a high school education came to be regarded as the birthright of anyone who was not a positive dullard. Poverty was not always a barrier – many students worked in their spare time or during vacations to earn the money for their schooling.

227

If American literature had its golden age in the years immediately preceding the Civil War, there was a 'silver age' of considerable talent in the 1920s. Experiments in verse ranged from the sardonic harshness of Edgar Lee Masters to the romantic enthusiasm of Vachel Lindsay. The best known, perhaps, of the new poets was Robert Frost, who celebrated the countryfolk 'north of Boston.' Edwin Arlington Robinson, a poet's poet, gained as much critical approval, if not so wide an audience. Amy Lowell of the imagist school made of verse a pictorial pattern. T S Eliot, author of *The Wasteland*, though born in the United States, spent his active years in England. Stephen Vincent Benét won a Pulitzer Prize for his epic of the Civil War, *John Brown's Body*.

Even more noteworthy were the laurels gathered by American writers of fiction. Sinclair Lewis, Pearl S Buck, William Faulkner, Ernest Hemingway and John Steinbeck gained Nobel Prizes in this field, as did the somber Eugene O'Neill in drama. All were critical realists. There was a noteworthy output of biography, but it seemed (at least during the 1920s) most popular

Opposite far left: Mary Pickford, the movie star, was called 'America's Sweetheart'. She is shown here with President Herbert Hoover. *Left:* William Faulkner, one of America's most prominent novelists, was awarded the Nobel Prize for Literature in 1949.

Opposite right center: Another Nobel Prize winner, in 1954, was Ernest Hemingway. *Opposite right below:* Stephen Vincent Benét was a poet and novelist whose most famous work was *John Brown's Body*. *Below:* Herbert Hoover, the thirty-first president of the United States.

when it was slightly cynical. A typical critic of the age was H L Mencken, who ridiculed almost everything American, from the complacent conservatives to the idealistic reformers.

But the foundations of the prosperous decade were insecure. There was much over-speculation on the stock exchange, and a roseate expectation that the days of depression had given way to 'a permanent plateau of prosperity.' The future was to show a very different face.

President Coolidge, who might easily have won another term, said in his laconic fashion, 'I do not choose to run,' and the succession fell to Herbert Hoover, the secretary of commerce, former mining engineer and wartime food administrator. He easily defeated Alfred E Smith, who won New England but could not hold the Solid South. For the first time since reconstruction, several former Confederate states broke from the Democratic ranks to protest the nomination of a candidate who was at once a 'wet,' a Roman Catholic and an associate of Tammany Hall. But Hoover had been in office scarcely seven months when the nation plunged into a prolonged economic depression.

THE GREAT DEPRESSION

Ever since Joseph prophesied to the Egyptian pharaoh that the fat kine would be followed by the lean kine, or in more modern terms a boom period would be followed by a depression, people have understood economic cycles. The United States had had major depressions in 1837, 1857, 1873 and 1893, as well as minor recessions. Each was acute for about three years and each had been preceded by a wave of speculations on the stock markets.

The depression which hit the United States in 1929 was more severe and extensive than any of these, mainly because the nation had become more completely industrialized. Farmers are affected by the state of the market, but there is always some demand for food and, at worst, the farmers can raise their own. But when John Citizen says to his wife, 'My dear, we can't afford that new car this year,' a factory closes down and hundreds of unemployed are turned into the street. This, in turn, reduces effective demand and slows industry yet more.

One of the main causes of the depression was of European origin. Recovery from World War I had been slow and only partial. Europeans could neither buy American goods nor pay back war loans to the United States. In several foreign countries the currency had been inflated beyond recovery. The consequent dislocation of international trade was bound to affect the United States adversely. Another key factor was the over-production of consumer goods in the United States for which the market had dried up.

In October 1929 a panic hit Wall Street. In three days an estimated 15 billion dollars in market values had been wiped out in frantic selling and, by the end of the year, some 40 billion. An unemployment census in 1930 reported 3 million of the usually employed to be out of work; in 1932 the number had soared to an estimated 15 million.

Attempts were made, of course, to hold off the panic by leading politicians and financiers who made reassuring statements. They agreed that the nation was 'fundamentally sound,' that the ruin of a few speculators was not the ruin of the country, and that 'prosperity was just around the corner.' But it took a long time to turn that corner. Reverberations from Europe aggravated the American situation. National income dwindled from 81 billion dollars in 1929 to 41 billion in 1932.

When people have suffered severe economic loss they are apt to turn against any government then in power. The European depression brought Hitler into power in Germany and deposed the King in Spain. The United States has always escaped revolution, but it is notable that each great depressions has been followed at the next general election by political reversal. In 1840 the Democrats suffered their first defeat in four decades when the Whigs elected William Henry 'Tippecanoe' Harrison. In 1860 the Republicans first came into power; in 1876 the Democrats were so close to winning that the result hung in doubt long after the election; in 1896 the Republicans displaced the Democrats.

The depression made a Democratic victory in 1932 inevitable. President Hoover was renominated but neither he nor his party had much hope for victory. The Democratic convention was a short but bitter contest between Al Smith, the nominee four years earlier, and Franklin D Roosevelt, who was easily nominated and elected. In 1928 Hoover had 21 million popular votes to Smith's 15 million and carried 40 states; in 1932 he had less than 16 million to Roosevelt's almost 23 million and carried only five states.

President Hoover had taken some measures to fight the depression. He instituted a Reconstruction Finance Corporation to bolster weak links in the national economy. But he was fundamentally a self-made individualist and did not wish to take the federal government too deeply into the sphere of direct charity. By 1932 the United States was ready for far more drastic remedies.

Above: Black Tuesday. It was October 1929, when 16.4 million shares changed hands, and the bottom dropped out of the market. *Top right:* Thousands of people were left without work and many had no food to eat. *Right:* Destitute men in Washington DC stand in line to receive relief packages at the Central Union Mission, 1930.

Left: Bread lines stretched for blocks in many parts of the country. This scene was photographed at the corner of Sixth Avenue and 42nd Street in New York City in February 1932. *Above:* Hunger marches were organized protesting the lack of government help in providing food for out-of-work people. This march took place in Washington DC 6 December 1931. *Right:* In the mid-1930s came the mass exodus from the Dust Bowl to the West Coast. A picture of a family from Missouri that was entitled by the photographer, *Broke, Sick Baby, Car Trouble.* John Steinbeck chronicled the plight of these 'Okies' in his novel *The Grapes of Wrath.*

Top: Tenant farmers in Chatham, North Carolina, 1939. *Above:* Those fortunate enough to find some agricultural work often had to live in horrible shacks (Oklahoma City, July 1939). *Right:* An abandoned farm in the middle of the Dust Bowl (Oklahoma 1936).

FRANKLIN ROOSEVELT AND HIS NEW DEAL

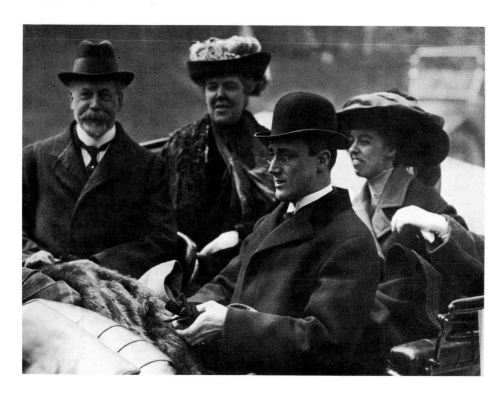

Left: Franklin Delano and Eleanor Roosevelt with Mr and Mrs Henry Parrish at Hyde Park, New York, 1913. It was during that year that he was elected to his second term in the New York Senate and President Wilson appointed him an Assistant Secretary of the Navy. *Below:* Roosevelt as Assistant Secretary of the Navy, 1913. *Right:* Works Progress Administration (WPA) workers grade three runways at the Charlotte, North Carolina airport, April 1936. *Overleaf:* WPA workers loading a truck with food debris – Louisville, February 1937.

Theodore and Franklin Roosevelt were second cousins, and their careers showed some remarkable parallels. Both had been assistant secretaries of the navy, both were governors of New York, both had been candidates for vice president – Theodore successfully, Franklin unsuccessfully. Both had the reputation of belonging to the liberal, or reformist wing of their respective parties, but both were more opportunistic than ideological and showed more political adroitness than logical consistency.

Their chief difference was not that one was a Republican and the other a Democrat, but that Theodore lived in quiet times until he made them stirring by his own strenuous activity; whereas Franklin had to wrestle with a world depression and a world war. There is some chance that history may call both Roosevelts 'born great,' but Theodore also 'achieved greatness,' while Franklin had his 'thrust upon him' by a great crisis.

During his campaign for the presidency in 1932 Roosevelt did not spell out the details of his recovery program; perhaps he had not yet clearly formulated it in his own mind. Certainly many people thought, as did Walter Lippmann, that this quiet, amiable man was no 'tribune of the people' and 'no enemy of entrenched privilege.' Furthermore, Roosevelt had been crippled by an attack of polio which had almost forced him out of politics.

In his inaugural address Roosevelt sounded a note of confidence. He pointed out that American resources were as great as ever and that the nation had 'nothing to fear but fear itself'. During his so-called 'hundred days' he urged Congress to adopt an unprecedented number of emergency measures. Collectively these were called the New Deal from a phrase of Mark Twain's, although it reminded some people of Theodore Roosevelt's Square Deal and Wilson's New Freedom.

To provide jobs for the unemployed he suggested the Works Projects Administration (WPA); the Public Works Administration (PWA) and the Civilian Conservation Corps (CCC). The National Recovery Act (NRA) had a broader aim, to organize a code of fair practice for each industry, shorten the work week, ban child labor and establish minimum wages. The Agricultural Adjustment Administration (AAA) attempted to raise farm prices by restricting crops and slaughtering excess pigs. Both of these comprehensive measures were declared unconstitutional by the Supreme Court as exceeding the powers of Congress. To raise prices the gold content

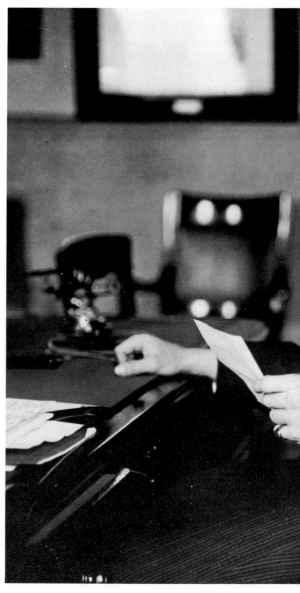

of the dollar was decreased and the United States (as had already happened in several European countries) was placed on a paper currency basis.

About the only experiment in actual government ownership was the Tennessee Valley Authority (TVA), which involved public generation of electricity in open competition with private power. Congress ended prohibition and cancelled the national regulation of the liquor industry.

Obviously, changes so many and so great were bound to cause a reaction. Conservative former Democrats, including their national candidates in the previous elections, Davis and Smith, seceded from the party. A 'Liberty League' was organized to oppose Roosevelt's liberalism (not the only time in American history when contending factions have both appealed to 'liberty'). When Roosevelt tried to override the decisions of the Supreme Court by enlarging the court and thus giving the president a chance to appoint new men, Congress balked on the grounds that this might undermine the independence of the judicial branch of the government. It was the president's first major defeat. Later, however, deaths and resignations of some judges and the shift in opinion of others enabled Roosevelt to achieve his aim by other means.

He had adversaries from the Left as well as the Right. Not only the Socialist and Communist Parties, whose opposition might be expected, but there was also a strange catch-all Union Party led by Gerald L K Smith of the old Huey Long machine in Louisiana; Father Coughlin, a priest who broadcast on the radio, once a friend to Roosevelt and now a bitter enemy; and Dr Francis Townsend, who had his own pet scheme for old age pensions, the money to be rapidly spent to stimulate commerce.

In spite of these defections, Roosevelt was easily re-elected over Governor Alfred Landon of Kansas, the Republican nominee. In a sweep, as unexpected to the victors as to the vanquished, Roosevelt carried 46 states, leaving only Maine and Vermont obdurate. The depression was not quite over, but the recovery was sufficiently marked to give Roosevelt an unprecedented triumph.

The Democrats had achieved a new majority by putting together their three traditional elements (the Solid South, the party machines in the urban East and the rural radicals of the West) with the bulk of the poor, the foreign born ethnics and the Blacks, hitherto Republican, but grateful for new jobs.

EUROPE'S ROAD TO WAR

Had it not been for the Second World War, Franklin Roosevelt would have been content with two terms, a precedent never before broken. But in 1939 and 1940 Germany had wiped Poland from the map, overwhelmed France and occupied Belgium, Holland, Denmark and Norway. Italy and Japan, Germany's foes in World War I, were now allied with her. Germany, unable to conquer Britain by sea, struck at her by air in nightly raids.

The United States was again, as during Napoleon's and Kaiser Wilhelm's time, the leading neutral. But popular sentiment was now very different. For the first time, Americans felt directly imperiled. In 1914 there was a line of French and British troops, as well as the British Navy, between the United States and danger. Now, the first wall of defense had gone down and the second was in danger. Moreover, many German-Americans who could tolerate the Kaiser were alienated by the fanaticism of Adolph Hitler.

Even before the war the aggressions of the Axis Powers (Germany, Italy and Japan) had alarmed Americans: Germany had annexed Austria and Czechoslovakia; Italy took Ethiopia and Albania; Japan occupied Korea, Manchuria and the Chinese coast. When war broke out, American sympathies were obviously on the side of the victimized nations. Yet there was still much objection to intervention; The America First organization pointed out that the First World War had wholly failed to achieve Wilson's aim 'to make the world safe for democracy.' A popular saying was that it had brought nothing to the United States except 'bad debts, influenza and prohibition.'

Below: Hitler believed that Germans, as members of the master race, had superior rights. The 'Nordic', or 'Aryan', race, of whom the Germans were held to be the only really pure strain, were born to command. All other races were born to take orders. Mixture with 'impure' blood was an affront to the race. The Jews, of all people, were the most inferior, he thought. *Right:* A conference during the Appeasement at Munich. Left to right: Benito Mussolini, Hitler, Dr Paul Schmidt (Hitler's chief interpreter) and Neville Chamberlain. Representatives of four nations – Great Britain, France, Germany and Italy – met at Munich, 29 September 1938 to buy peace at the expense of Czechoslovakia. *Opposite below:* Hitler reviews some troops who are on their way to Poland, 21 September 1939.

On the other hand, William Allen White, the Kansas editor, headed a Committee to Defend America by Aiding the Allies. The Roosevelt administration took several steps to give the British 'every aid short of war,' in spite of the Neutrality Acts of the 1930s.

Munitions might be sent to belligerents in their merchant ships for prompt payment (Cash and Carry). The American government was later authorized to 'lend' munitions of war to belligerents (Lend-Lease). A number of destroyers were given to the British in exchange for the right to naval bases on British possessions in the Western Hemisphere. All these measures were deliberate attempts to aid one side against the other. The United States even adopted military conscription, a step never previously taken except during the Civil War and World War I.

In 1940 the Republicans nominated Wendell Willkie, a popular industrialist who had never held political office. His foreign policy did not differ greatly from that of Roosevelt, although he was more conservative on domestic issues. Franklin Roosevelt decided to run for a third term. Again he was elected, though some of the farm states swung back into the Republican column.

Below: Paris fell to the Germans 14 June 1940, and soon German troops were seen everywhere. *Right:* 85 Squadron of the Royal Air Force flying their Hawker Hurricanes during the Battle of Britain, 1940. *Below:* The 51st Highland Division surrenders at St Valery-en-Caux 12 June 1940. Gen Erwin Rommel stands beside captured British officers. *Far right below:* Emergency air raid shelters were set up in the London Underground. *Overleaf:* A scene on the Western Desert in September 1942.

JAPAN STRIKES WITHOUT WARNING

The warlords of Japan had an opportunity which they could not resist. Great Britain, the mistress of the seas, had to keep her navy in European waters for self-defense. France and Holland, also interested in Pacific affairs, had been occupied by Germany. Russia was fighting for its life on the German front. During the 1930s Japan had occupied Manchuria and the Chinese coast, and now no power on earth except the United States could interpose itself between Japan and a potential empire over all eastern Asia and the Pacific island world.

If the American Pacific fleet could be destroyed, this last barrier would be gone. But to do this required a sudden and secret attack. So, while American peace negotiations with Japan were still proceeding in Washington in the hope of ending the war between China and Japan, a combined Japanese sea and air force struck at Pearl Harbor in Hawaii.

Early Sunday morning, 7 December 1941, which President Roosevelt termed 'a day that will live in infamy,' the Japanese attacked the American Pacific Fleet and severely damaged it. By this act of treachery Japan had won at a stroke her open door to an empire.

Of course, Congress responded with an immediate declaration of war, opposed by only one pacifist from Montana. Had the United States, as at one time seemed probable, gradually waded into the war, there would have been, as on former occasions, some difference of opinion. But the manner of the Japanese assault ended all debate.

Germany backed Japan by declaring war on the United States, thus merging the European and Far Eastern wars. Once again, America was a belligerent in a World War, aided by Hitler's rash decision simultaneously to take on Russia, the British Empire and the United States. Winston Churchill was probably right in thinking that this was the turning point of World War II; once again the Germans had underestimated the military potential of both English-speaking countries. Nevertheless, the immediate effect of the treacherous attack was a long succession of disasters for American and British forces.

Below: Japanese naval aircraft ready to take off for Pearl Harbor from an aircraft carrier 7 December 1941. *Right:* A view of Pearl Harbor looking to the southwest, two months before the Japanese attack. *Opposite below:* American defenders at Hickam Field.

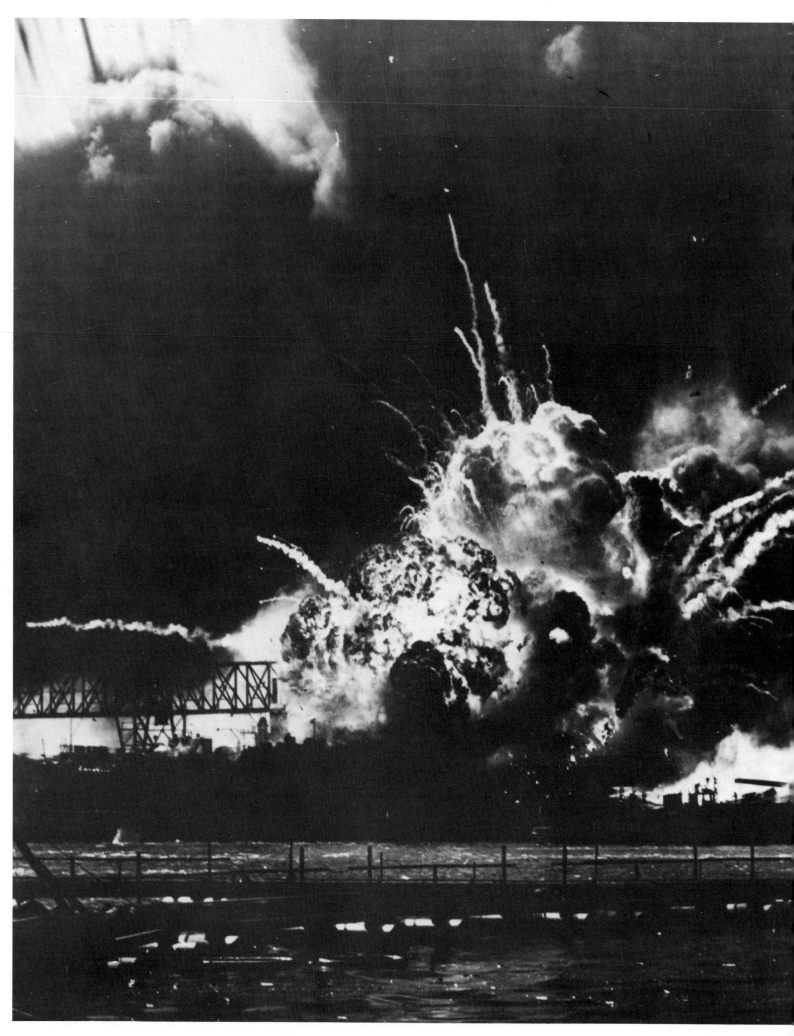

Left: The magazine of the destroyer *USS Shaw* explodes during the Japanese attack. *Above:* A view of the destruction in the harbor. *Right:* The *USS Nevada* under attack. This battleship would later be rebuilt and would rejoin the fleet before the war was over.

Left: Part of the devastation at Pearl Harbor. The *USS Downes* is in front, with the *USS Cassin* behind it. At the rear is the *USS Pennsylvania. Right:* Newspapers all over the country published extra editions following the attack.

THE SECOND WORLD WAR

The Japanese followed up their initial advantage, seizing Wake and Midway Islands, advancing even to the outlying Alaskan Aleutian Islands and forcing General Douglas MacArthur from the Philippines. The British lost the ports of Hong Kong and Singapore, Malaya and many Pacific islands; the French lost Indo-China; the Dutch lost Indonesia. Burma was occupied, as was independent Thailand (Siam). India and Australia were threatened, although not actually invaded. No nation had ever gained so much so speedily.

President Roosevelt made the difficult decision to give priority to the European war. Germany had advanced to the very gates of Moscow and Leningrad and seized oil wells in the Caucasus. If either Britain or Russia should break, the war might be lost. Roosevelt worked closely with British Prime Minister Winston Churchill in a long series of diplomatic and military conferences. Joseph Stalin, the Russian dictator, was driven to temporary partnership by the pressing danger from Hitler, and Churchill, a foe of Bolshevism, said, 'If Hitler declares war on Hell, I will try to find something good to say about the Devil!'

The Free French under General Charles De Gaulle still kept up a resistance in Africa even after France had surrendered. So the reconquest began there. While the Russians held firm at Stalingrad, the British kept their hold on Egypt and American and British forces invaded French North Africa, then under the control of the Nazi-oriented Vichy regime.

The periodic panic, during which residents of Japanese ancestry were moved from the Pacific coast and resettled inland, soon passed. Step by step, the Pacific islands were retaken. Combined air, sea and land forces in New Guinea, Okinawa, Guadalcanal and elsewhere pushed back the Japanese, who were now on the defensive.

Right: The wartime gas shortage. Not only was gasoline rationed, but also many service stations cut down on their hours of operation. *Below:* One of the shames of the war: American residents of Japanese ancestry, many of them citizens, were rounded up and sent to internment camps. *Opposite below:* Show business personalities did their bit for the war effort – rounding up metal utensils at the Stork Club in New York. Merle Oberon is third from the right.

Opposite top: Marlene Dietrich in Cleveland 19 June 1942. She was on a nation-wide tour promoting the sale of war bonds. *Left:* Servicemen being entertained at the Hotel Lexington in New York City 30 December 1941. *Top:* The crew of the B-17 'Flying Fortress', *The Memphis Belle,* back from their 25th mission in June 1943. *Above:* Roosevelt and Churchill during a press conference at their Casablanca meeting, 24 January 1943.

British and American armies slowly reconquered Italy. Premier Benito Mussolini was overthrown and later murdered by Italian insurgents. At last a vast army under the American general, Dwight D Eisenhower, performed that most difficult of all military operations – a landing in force on a defended coast – and invaded Normandy.

In a few months' time, France was completely cleared of the occupying German forces and, in turn, Germany was invaded. The Americans seized the Remagen bridgehead and passed the Rhine River. In the meantime, the Russians had reconquered all their lost soil and invaded the Balkans. It was obvious that the war had been won, the only question that remained was how quickly it could be brought to a conclusion.

In 1944 Roosevelt ran for an unprecedented fourth term against Governor Thomas E Dewey of New York. He was reelected but close observers could see that his health had been undermined by the prolonged strain of war leadership. He died at the health resort of Warm Springs, Georgia and was succeeded by Vice President Harry S Truman of Missouri.

To Truman there came the momentous decision – whether or not to drop the atomic bomb on Japan. Before this, explosives merely released the atoms from unstable molecules. Now the new weapon involved the release of forces within unstable atoms such as one form of uranium. For months the problem had been studied on American soil by a group of physicists from several nations (the Manhattan Project). An experimental bomb had been exploded in New Mexico and was then used against the Japanese ports of Hiroshima and Nagasaki. A single explosion of the new weapon was as destructive as one hundred air raids with conventional weapons.

There was no general peace conference after the Second World War as there had been after the First. Germany, the chief belligerent, was jointly occupied by Russian, British, American and French forces. Hitler had committed suicide in a Berlin air-raid shelter, but a few other Nazi leaders were brought to trial for war offences against humanity. A few Japanese leaders were executed. Russia reclaimed Sakhalin and the Kuriles from Japan; China, Manchuria and Formosa (Taiwan); Korea, under temporary Russian and American occupation, was nominally independent.

Left: Omaha Beach, 6 June 1944. American troops are digging in. *Right:* A three-man combat patrol in Belgium 11 September 1944. They are in advance of the main force holding Battice, a few miles to the rear.

The United States had been involved in World War I from April 1917 to November 1918 – in World War II from December 1941 until the surrender of Japan in August 1945, more than twice as long. In the former, some 4 million young men had been called to the colors and over 50 thousand were killed in battle. In the latter, 16 million were sworn in and nearly 300 thousand were killed in battle. In the former, American forces, with minor exceptions, were concentrated in Western Europe; in the latter, Americans fought in Africa, Italy, France, Belgium, Germany, the Philippines, Melanesia, Micronesia, Polynesia, China and Burma. But as the only great power which was not bombarded or invaded, the United States emerged from the Second World War as the mightiest of all the world powers.

Top left: An F6F about to take off from the flight deck of the *USS Yorktown*, 19 June 1944. *Left:* Mail was all-important to the fighting man. Mail call in St Lô, barely a week after the capture of the city. *Top right:* A crash landing of an F6F on the *USS*

Enterprise during the campaign in the Gilbert Islands. *Right:* Two marines using a flame-thrower against the Japanese defenses on Iwo Jima, 24 February 1945. *Overleaf:* A victory garden planted by New York schoolchildren.

TRUMAN AND EISENHOWER

Like most vice presidents suddenly called to the presidency, Harry Truman was unprepared for his new responsibilities, but he faced his problems courageously and successfully engineered the ending of the war and the establishment of the United Nations as a successor to the late League of Nations. Far from refusing membership, as the United States had done in the case of the League, she became the main factor in the new organization and its center was located, not in far-off Geneva, but in New York City.

President Truman was faced by many problems including rampant postwar inflation and a crisis in housing, as 15 million men returned, often with their new brides, to find the only places that they could live in were Quonset or Nissen huts. Coal miners and railroad workers alike struck for higher wages and better working conditions.

Abroad, Truman was faced with the Communist takeover of most of Eastern Europe, which was followed in February 1948 by a Communist *coup d'état* in Czechoslovakia. Chiang Kai-shek's Kuomintang, America's nationalist ally in China, was losing its civil war to Mao Tse-tung's Communists.

In answer to these challenges, Truman threatened to nationalize both the coal and steel industries and faced down the labor union challenge. In his foreign policy, the Truman Doctrine was promulgated in which the United States took over Britain's role of supporting the forces of democracy in Greece and Turkey. But Truman came under heavy criticism for allowing China, as well as Czechoslovakia and other parts of Eastern Europe, to 'go down the drain.' In neither case could Truman have done very much without starting World War III.

Opposite top: Gen George
C Marshall was appointed
the US envoy to China
in 1945. He is shown
in Nanking with
Generalissimo Chiang
Kai-shek and Madame
Chiang. *Left:* Harry S
Truman holding aloft the
premature edition of *The
Chicago Tribune* that

announced Thomas E
Dewey's victory. *Top
right:* Harry S Truman.
the thirty-third president
of the United States, on
his whistle-stop campaign
of 1948. *Above:* The
millionth ton of Marshall
Plan food reached Greece
21 December 1949.

But it became clear in 1948 that the new president was being attacked by forces within his own party as well as by the Republicans, who had taken control of the Congress in 1946 and who were hoping to take the presidency in 1948.

Few expected that Truman could be elected on his own. The Democrats had suffered secessions both to the Right and to the Left; some southern states supported Strom Thurmond on a 'states rights' platform of white ascendancy; some radicals nominated Henry Wallace in a new Progressive Party demanding conciliation with Soviet Russia. 'How can a bird fly with both wings gone?' people asked, and expected an easy victory for Thomas E Dewey, again the Republican candidate.

To the surprise of nearly everyone, except perhaps for Harry himself, Truman was elected; a shift in some farm states brought him the necessary vote margin, and Wallace's Progressives, who had been expected to cut into his vote, did much less than half as well as had La Follette's Progressives in 1924, and were far outdistanced by Theodore Roosevelt's Progressives of 1912. One Conservative Democrat moaned, 'The Roosevelt revolution is still with us.' Truman had achieved what was almost a miracle at the polls. Against bookmakers' odds of 15 to 1, the Democrats won the presidency, swept both Houses of Congress and were back for another four years.

Truman's greatest challenge in 1949 was the growing Communist threat. In 1947 the secretary of state, George C Marshall, gave a speech at Harvard in which he enunciated his plan to rehabilitate Western Europe, a program which went into full swing in 1949 and was ever after referred to as the Marshall Plan.

Truman realized that an economically weak Europe would soon fall prey to the Communist challenge, and most of the major nations of Western Europe joined the United States and Canada in forming the North Atlantic Treaty Organization (NATO) in 1949. Then came the Korean War. A disillusioned nation turned to the Republican Party to end the war in Korea and to carry on the fight against the Communist enemy both at home and abroad.

The Republican victory expected in 1948, came in 1952. The nomination was contested between Senator Robert A Taft, son of the former president, a strong conservative and called by his friends 'Mr Republican' and General Dwight D Eisenhower, the chief American hero of the Second World War and called 'Ike' by his friends.

The Democrats nominated Adlai E Stevenson, the governor of Illinois, who accepted the nomination with some reluctance, aware of the odds against him. Eisenhower was elected by a landslide. He ended the Korean conflict and presided for eight years over a generally prosperous and peaceful country.

Below left: Eisenhower received 442 electoral votes to a mere 89 for Adlai E Stevenson in 1952. *Right:* Dwight D Eisenhower, the thirty-fourth president of the United States. *Below:* Richard M Nixon was selected as Eisenhower's running mate at the Republican National Convention of 1952.

Ike and Mamie read of General's smashing victory in NEWS at Hotel Commodore.—*Story p. 3; other pics, centerfold*

REPUBLICAN NATIONAL CON

THE KOREAN WAR

For a short time after the war with Japan, Russia occupied North Korea, and the United States South Korea. When the occupying forces were withdrawn they left a native Communist government in the former Russian zone and a non-Communist government in the American. All Koreans desired unity but the question was, which government would swallow the other?

The Soviet Union urged its North Korean puppet to attack South Korea, which it did in June 1950. General Douglas MacArthur sent American troops based in Japan into the war zone, striking north of the battle line and forcing the Communists to retreat rapidly. When they had retreated to the Yalu River, the boundary between Korea and Chinese Manchuria, Communist China became alarmed and sent hordes of 'volunteers' to aid the North Koreans.

Eventually the battle line was stabilized not far from the original political boundary between the two Koreas. MacArthur wished to push on to a complete victory, but Truman feared a general war with China, vetoed his policy and removed him from command.

The stalemate which occurred in the Korean peninsula and the dismissal of MacArthur came as a shock to Americans who had substituted the figures of Mao and Stalin in the demonology where once Hitler and Hirohito stood. Some Americans were disappointed, saying that it was the first time America had engaged in a war and had not won it, possibly forgetting the drawn war of 1812 with Great Britain. But President Eisenhower did not renew the conflict, and Korea remained divided between the two governments. Something similar but on a more important scale had happened in Germany.

Left: When Truman fired Gen Douglas MacArthur, it was headline news.
Right: Brig Gen Courtney Whitney, MacArthur and Maj Gen Edward M Almond observe the shelling of Inchon from the *USS Mt McKinley*, 15 September 1950.

Above: Truman's vice-president, Alben W Barkley, toured the Yonchon-Chorwon area of Korea.
Left to right: Barkley, Gen James A Van Fleet, Gen Thomas J Cross and Gen Matthew B Ridgway.
Below: Eating Thanksgiving dinner on the banks of the Yalu River in Korea 23 November 1950.
Right: An American and a Korean MP checking Korean refugees for smuggled weapons,
24 August 1950.

Above: A scout from the
23rd Infantry Regiment,
wounded on a patrol
mission, receives medical
attention, 14 February
1952. His partner, a ROK
soldier, was also wounded
and is being assisted up
the hill. *Left:* An

American squad in their winter camouflage uniforms, moves out, 1 January 1952. *Right:* Eisenhower promised during his 1952 campaign that he would visit Korea and end the war there.

THE COLD WAR WITH THE SOVIET UNION

The dictators of Soviet Russia had never trusted the United States, even when they were allies in World War II. It was a dogma with them that capitalist and communist countries could never really be friends. The break became acute in 1948. After World War II Germany had been divided into Russian, British, French and American zones. The Russians organized their part into the 'German Democratic Republic,' containing about one quarter of the area and population of the country. The rest became the 'German Federal Republic', with its capital at Bonn.

Berlin was jointly occupied, but it, too, became divided. West Berlin was a political island, surrounded by Communist territory. East Berlin was the capital of the Russian dominated German Democratic Republic, and the Communists made an attempt to starve out West Berlin, but this was foiled by an American airlift. Eventually the Communists sealed off East Berlin with a wall of concrete and barbed wire – ostensibly to keep invaders out, but actually to keep would-be emigrants in.

Russia outright annexed Lithuania, Latvia, Estonia and a small part of Finland. Communist governments were established in Poland, Czechoslovakia, Hungary, Romania, Albania and Bulgaria. Yugoslavia, too, turned Communist but refused Russian leadership.

This imposition of Communism by force caused dismay in western countries. There were two 'red scares' in the United States. One, in 1919–

Above: The Berlin Airlift began 26 June 1948. By the time it ceased operation 15 months later, more than 2 million tons of food supplies had been delivered in more than a quarter million flights. *Opposite top:* The Potsdamerplatz in Berlin, on the border between the East and West zones, was the scene of a number of East-West Berlin riots. East Berlin police are shown in a line, 16 March 1950, to keep their people in their East sector. *Right:* Two US Army officers (foreground) hold a street conference with two Russian officers (background) near the Potsdamerplatz.

20, involved the deportation to Russia of a number of alleged revolutionary radicals. The other, after 1948, caused an outcry against Communists alleged to have found their home in the Truman administration. Senator Joseph McCarthy of Wisconsin accused those whose politics he disliked of being 'card-carrying Communists,' although he was totally unable to bring proof to support his charges. When McCarthy attacked the army he ran afoul of President Eisenhower and was condemned by the Senate. His early death removed him from the political scene.

Senator Richard Nixon of California had more success. His investigations did turn up some suspicious characters such as Alger Hiss, an achievement which helped lead to his nomination as Eisenhower's vice president.

Encouraged by many politicians, including Vice President Richard M Nixon and Senate Majority Leader Lyndon B Johnson, to aid the French in their attempt to retain Indochina under their colonial control, Eisenhower wisely chose not to intervene in 1954. The French regime fell and a communist government was established in North Vietnam.

Secretary of State John Foster Dulles helped to create a Southeast Asia Treaty Organization (SEATO) which was meant to defend the rest of Indochina. The United States was joined by its ANZUS allies, Australia, and New Zealand, as well as Britain, France, the Philippines, Thailand and

Pakistan, which was a signatory to the CENTO, or Baghdad, Pact of which Turkey was also a member. Thus by 1954 the Soviet Union and Communist China were surrounded by a series of alliances all linked directly or indirectly to the United States, including Japan, South Korea and Taiwan (all that was left of Nationalist China after the fall of China to the Communists in 1949). Secretary Dulles' containment policy was seen as a deterrent to further Communist aggression.

Left: British tanks in the streets during the Suez invasion by Britain, France and Israel. *Below:* Secretary of State John Foster Dulles met with Philippine President Ramon Magsaysay in Manila 21 February 1955, when Dulles was en route to Bangkok for a SEATO donverence. *Right:* Senator Joseph McCarthy of Wisconsin during the televised Army-McCarthy hearings 22 April–17 June 1954. At the left is lawyer Joseph Welsh. McCarthy was condemned by the Senate 2 December for his actions. *Opposite below:* The opening session of a SEATO conference. Dean Acheson is seated second from left and Dulles is second from right.

But in 1956, a week before the election in which Eisenhower won a second term against his 1952 rival, Adlai Stevenson, the Soviet Union crushed a quasi-democratic movement in Hungary under the leadership of Imre Nagy, while at the same time Britain, France and Israel attacked Egypt. Eisenhower stood aloof from both conflicts, thereby temporarily alienating Britain and France, but avoiding any direct American involvement either in the Middle East or in Eastern Europe.

Soon afterward, he promulgated the Eisenhower Doctrine which was meant to protect any nation in the Middle East against direct aggression, and the United States Marines briefly entered Lebanon in 1958 to give strength to his policy.

As a result of his cautious but forceful actions, aggression was kept to a minimum during the 1950s while the United States enjoyed an unprecedented period of prosperity. The Blacks, under the leadership of Dr Martin Luther King, JR, pressured the Eisenhower administration into enacting two Civil Rights bills in 1957 and 1958. Eisenhower appointed troops to enforce integration of the schools of Little Rock, Arkansas despite the intransigence of the governor, Orville Faubus.

Eisenhower could have run again for president and won easily were it not for the 22nd amendment to the Constitution which forbade any president to run more than twice – an amendment that was enacted during the time of the Truman administration. So Eisenhower stepped down in favor of his vice president, Richard M Nixon, who ran against Senator John F Kennedy of Massachusetts in 1960.

Below: The 'Kitchen Debate' in Moscow, 1959, between Prime Minister Nikita Khrushchev and Richard M Nixon. *Right:* The Berlin Wall with its 'no man's land' between the fences. *Opposite below:*

A platoon of US Marines, who had served as security troops in Lebanon, marching to the dock where they will board ships to take them back to the fleet, 15 August 1958.

JOHN KENNEDY

In 1960 John F Kennedy narrowly defeated Nixon for president. Kennedy, like Alfred E Smith, was a Roman Catholic, but he encountered less hostility on that account. This was not only because the nation had grown more tolerant, but also because Senator Kennedy, a brisk young Harvard graduate and author of several books, did not carry with him the taint of Tammany Hall or the city docksides. Kennedy won by a whisker in the closest election since 1892.

Kennedy was America's youngest elected president and his youth was challenged by an unsuccessful attempt to overthrow Fidel Castro in Cuba, who had taken power in 1959 and soon after proclaimed himself a Communist.

Russia's premier Nikita Khrushchev, having met Kennedy in the spring of 1961 in Vienna, thought little of him and challenged his experience by building the Berlin Wall in June of 1961. Believing he could get away with anything, Khrushchev placed Soviet missiles in Cuba in 1962 and Kennedy was forced to meet the challenge. As Russian ships with missiles bound for Havana steamed toward the Cuban shore, Kennedy interdicted the Russian fleet with an American naval blockade of Cuba. The Russian ships turned away, thereby averting the greatest threat to peace since 1945 and avoiding an almost certain world conflict which would have ensued had the Russians pushed their luck.

Kennedy's achievements were limited, and what he would have accomplished as president must remain unknown, for on 22 November 1963 he was shot and killed on a visit to Dallas, Texas. Since the assassin himself was shot before he could be brought to trial, his motives are not known and a mystery has surrounded Kennedy's assassination to this day, although some suspected that it was in Castro's interest.

Right: John F Kennedy, the Senator from Massachusetts and Democratic nominee for president in 1960, campaigning in Texas.

Left: For the first time in history, the nominee of the Republican and Democratic Parties debated on television. The moderator of the debate, seated on the dais between Kenney and Nixon, is Howard K Smith. *Right:* Kennedy toured Europe in 1961 and was greeted by Soviet Prime Minister Khrushchev in Vienna.

278

Opposite top: President Kennedy riding in the motorcade in Dallas, approximately one minute before he was shot 22 November 1963. *Left:* The funeral procession of President John F Kennedy.

Above: Seconds after her husband was shot, Jacqueline Kennedy leaned over him to protect him. *Right:* The slain president's brother, Robert, kneels at his grave 22 November 1964.

LYNDON JOHNSON

On the death of Kennedy, Vice President Lyndon B Johnson was his successor. He was a Texan and the first southerner to become president since Andrew Johnson of Tennessee (Woodrow Wilson was born in Virginia but his active career centered in New Jersey), and both Johnsons succeeded an assassinated president. Unlike most politicians from the Deep South, he had no racial prejudices and in his time Congress passed the most important legislation on behalf of the black population since

Below left: Lyndon Baines Johnson, the thirty-sixth president of the United States, succeeded Kennedy upon his death. He ran on his own in 1964, and was elected. *Right:* Johnson pulling the ears of his pet Beagle 'Him' at the LBJ ranch in Texas, 1964. *Opposite below:* Johnson taking the oath of office on board Air Force One following the death of President Kennedy.

ELECTION FINAL

DAILY ☆ NEWS
NEW YORK'S PICTURE NEWSPAPER ®

7¢
10¢ OUTSIDE L I AND SUBURBS

Vol. 46. No. 113 Copt 1964 News Syndicate Co. Inc.　New York, N.Y. 10017, Wednesday, November 4, 1964★　WEATHER: Sunny and pleasant.

LBJ WINS BIG

Kennedy Senator, Swamps Keating

Reconstruction days. Most of his desired laws were passed in the first nine months of his administration, and had already been envisaged by Kennedy.

His program for the so-called Great Society, in which he hoped to create social justice and full employment, was partly frustrated by deep involvement in a war in Vietnam, a part of the old French colony of Indochina. Had the war been successful it might have added to his prestige, but it dragged on inconclusively until the nation became deeply resentful.

Faced by a wave of unrest caused partly by the draft, or Selective Service Act, partly by the stalemated war in Vietnam, and with difficulties arising from the racial collision between militant Blacks and the white backlash, Johnson decided, to everyone's surprise, not to run again in 1968. This left the field open to several Democratic aspirants. Chief among them was Robert Kennedy, brother of the late president, who, in turn, was assassinated by an Arab fanatic.

Indeed, there was a regular epidemic of political assassinations; besides Robert Kennedy, there was Martin Luther King, the best-known champion of black rights; Malcolm X, a Black militant leader; George Lincoln Rockwell, the leader of the small faction of American Nazis;

and the near fatal shooting of Governor George Wallace of Alabama, who was running for the Democratic presidential nomination.

Vice President Hubert H Humphrey, a life-long liberal, was handicapped by the almost impossible task of keeping the support of Lyndon Johnson, under whom he had been vice president, and at the same time disassociating himself from Johnson's war policy. Nixon, the Republican candidate, expected an easy victory. But Humphrey came from behind and, by election day, almost closed the gap between the two parties. Nixon and his vice president, Spiro Agnew, entered office to take charge of a nation at war in Vietnam, and at war with itself.

Opposite far left: Vice-president Hubert H Humphrey in a moment of exuberance. *Left:* President Johnson in a serious moment. *Above:* Johnson was extremely proud of his LBJ Ranch. *Right:* Senator Robert F Kennedy of New York was shot in the Ambassador Hotel in Los Angeles, 5 June 1968, while campaigning for the Democratic nomination for president. He died the next day.

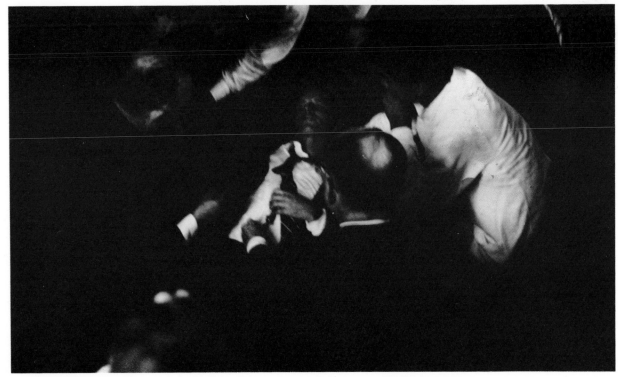

THE SECOND BLACK EMANCIPATION

In 1954 the Supreme Court unanimously ruled that racial segregation in the public schools violated the equal rights provisions of the 14th amendment. When, in 1957, Governor Orville Faubus of Arkansas called out guardsmen to prevent Blacks from entering an all-white public school, President Eisenhower sent federal troops to enforce the orders of the courts.

Voting rights, supposedly conferred by the 15th amendment, had long been evaded in the Deep South by various devices, such as literacy tests and poll taxes administered by white officials. Now, legislation brought cases of alleged discrimination before the federal courts and a series of Civil Rights bills was passed.

Desegregation in the schools had two effects. It led, in some southern states, to an exodus of well-to-do white children to private schools, and in the North to busing children from the Black Ghetto to schools in the white areas.

A series of demonstrations against racial discrimination in public buses and restaurants, joined not only by Blacks but also by sympathetic whites, undermined social discrimination. Quite outside the sphere of law, there were two other integrations. Athletic teams, both amateur and professional, admitted black players, who not infrequently became stars. Advertisements, in recognition of the buying power of prosperous Blacks, became careful to include them in group photographs in magazines and on television.

In 1968, the Reverend Martin Luther King, JR, the most conspicuous of the civil rights leaders, was assassinated. He was never an advocate of violence, as were some of the more extreme militants such as the Black Panthers. In some parts of the country an annual commemoration day was held in his honor. His movement lost force after his death, but much had been achieved, as Blacks won equality before the law in subsequent years. Although his dream of full equality was not achieved, a giant step was taken toward that goal.

Above: National Guard troops protecting the right of black children to enroll in Little Rock High School in Arkansas in 1954. The school had been ordered to integrate. *Left:* Gov Orval E Faubus of Arkansas, who attempted to block the integration of Little Rock. *Opposite top:* Blacks clashing with police in Birmingham, Alabama, 1963. *Right:* Dogs were used for crowd control during the Birmingham riots.

Left: The civil rights rally in Washington DC, 28 August, 1963, where Dr Martin Luther King Jr made his 'I Have a Dream' speech. *Above:* Dr Martin Luther King Jr, the 1964 winner of the Nobel Prize for Peace. *Top right:* The civil rights march in Montgomery, Alabama. *Right:* Dr King, flanked by Jesse Jackson and Ralph Abernathy, on the balcony of the Memphis Motel at approximately the spot where he would be shot the following day.

THE VIETNAM WAR

When France lost Indochina, that eastern empire fell apart into three states: Vietnam, Cambodia and Laos. In Vietnam two governments struggled for ascendancy; as in Korea, the North was Communist, the South was not. Fearing a 'domino effect' of repercussions in Indonesia and Malaya, the United States sent arms and military advisors to the southern government. Lyndon Johnson went further and committed over a half million American troops to the resistance.

This was a somewhat dubious venture. An Asiatic jungle war between two regimes, both dictatorial, was an unprecedented extension of the long arm of America. In Korea, at least, the United States had the backing of a United Nations resolution, though the military burden fell almost wholly on the United States. There was no declaration of war, although Congress, in a sense, authorized executive action by a resolution when American ships were attacked in the Gulf of Tonkin.

Of course, neither the Korean War nor the Vietnam conflicts were on a scale comparable to the Second World War, but they can scarcely be called minor wars, since Korea cost the United States over 30 thousand battle deaths and Vietnam nearly 50 thousand. Communist intrusions into Laos and Cambodia, plus American counterattacks, brought Laos and Cambodia into the war as well. When the United States finally pulled out, nearly the whole of Indochina was communist-dominated. Possibly even more important was the effect of the increasingly unpopular war on the youth movement in the United States.

Left: US riflemen charging Viet Cong positions in Vietnam. *Above:* Members of the 1st ARVN Division board helicopters in the A Shau Valley. *Top right:* A gunner on a rescue helicopter. *Right:* An American corporal of the 1st Cavalry Division takes time out from combat patrols.

Opposite top: An F-100 Super Sabre attacks a Viet Cong target, 1965. *Left:* Members of the 151st Ranger Infantry open fire against the enemy, 1969. *Right:* An American infantryman in Vietnam.

Left: Waiting for the helicopter to carry away the battle dead, 1966. *Below left:* President Nixon greets members of the 1st Infantry Division during his 1969 tour of Vietnam. *Right:* South Vietnamese being hurried off a helicopter during evacuation exercises, April 1975. *Below right:* South Vietnamese forces following terrified children, 8 June 1972, after an accidental aerial napalm attack. The girl at the center had ripped off her burning clothing.

THE YOUTH MOVEMENT

The Youth Movement may have begun with the 'Flaming Youth' of the 'Roaring Twenties,' but the new-found freedom of these young people soon became submerged in the face of the Great Depression. It was not until the 1960s that the Youth Movement became important again. Some young people took time out to join the Peace Corps and spent a few years serving abroad in impoverished parts of the world. Others took part in demonstrations for human rights: helping Blacks, particularly in the South, to be permitted to register to vote, or marched in support of civil rights. Some organized protests against the Vietnam War.

There was a dark underside to the Youth Movement. Although the 'hippies' and 'flower children' of the 'beat generation' were peaceable enough, wanting only to do their own thing without outside interference, some of them became revolutionaries. During the 1960s juvenile crime increased, the sale and use of drugs proliferated, and such anarchistic groups as the Weathermen made bombs and blew up buildings.

The Vietnam War became the focus of the youth rebellion. Some young men had fled to Canada to escape the draft. Anti-war riots on many college campuses resulted in burned or bombed buildings, sit-in occupations of administration buildings and occasionally the forceful detention of school officials. At Kent State University in Ohio in 1970, four students were shot and killed by members of a poorly disciplined National Guard unit during a protest.

Below: A youth rally protesting the Vietnam War and the Nixon administration, and supporting the Viet Cong and civil rights. *Right:* Another view of the same rally in Washington DC.

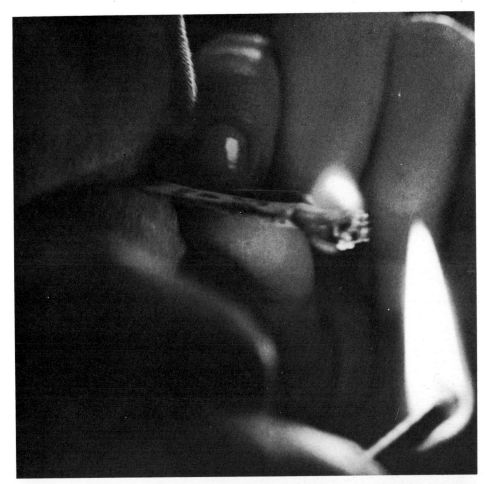

Left: An anti-Communist demonstration in New York City. *Right:* A youthful pot smoker draws on the remainder of a joint. *Below:* A policeman attempts to break up a 'POThibition' rally on a university campus.

Left: Police and a picket line. *Below:* Police charging student demonstrators at the University of California, Berkeley.

It may have been that the Youth Movement was a factor in Hubert H Humphrey's loss in the Presidential Election of 1968. At the time of the Democratic Convention in Chicago there was a series of confrontations between the police and the young war protesters that left such a bad impression of the Democrats that many people switched sides and voted for Richard Nixon.

The ending of the draft and America's involvement in Vietnam coupled with the recession created by the Mideast Crisis of 1973 caused the rapid decline of the protest movement. Young people became more concerned about their job prospects; many simply gave up. But the long-term impact of the youth protest and drug culture born in the 1960s has yet to be fully assessed or understood.

NIXON AND FORD

Below: Richard M Nixon and his running mate, Spiro T Agnew, accept their nomination at the Republican convention, 1968. *Bottom:* Nixon on the campaign trail. *Right:* Nixon and his wife, Pat, receiving a ticker-tape welcome in New York.

Richard Nixon tried to find a solution to the Vietnam imbroglio. He suggested the gradual withdrawal of American troops, but with the concomitant building up of the native South Vietnamese army, in order that Communism might not win a victory. He was the president when the Americans first stepped on the moon. Secure in his reputation as an unrelenting foe of Communism, he was able to reopen negotiations with Communist China.

In 1972 Nixon, because of the massive economic drain of the Great Society and the Vietnam War, floated the dollar, ending the relationship between gold and the dollar. The result was a huge devaluation of the dollar against most European currencies. In 1972 the Democrats nominated the liberal George McGovern of South Dakota to face Nixon in his reelection bid. Nixon nearly swept the board, carrying all electoral votes except those of Massachusetts and the District of Columbia.

But the second term of Nixon, like that of many two-term presidents, was filled with trouble. His vice president, Spiro Agnew, was accused of dishonesty by taking kickbacks and resigned under fire. Under the new constitutional arrangements, he appointed Gerald Ford of Michigan to fill the vacant post.

A much more serious matter was the threat to impeach President Nixon himself. This was partly the result of the so-called Watergate affair – a clumsy attempt secretly to bug a building occupied by Democratic campaign headquarters. Nixon did not himself contrive this, but he tried to hush it up and kept in office those who were really guilty. Moreover, as his private tapes proved, he had lied to the public as to the date when he found out about the matter.

There were also other unwarranted extensions of executive power. Nearly all seem to have been caused by Nixon's secretive disposition. Threatened with impeachment, Nixon retired to private life – the only president in American history to resign.

Gerald Ford assumed the presidency. He had a challenger in the primaries in 1976, Ronald Reagan of California, who objected to the returning of political control of the Panama Canal strip to the Panamanians. Ford was nominated, but was defeated by the Democratic candidate, Jimmy Carter of Georgia, who had attacked Ford's pardon of Nixon.

The fall of South Vietnam to the Communists was probably inevitable, but it helped to weaken Ford. Carter seemed the fresher of the two candidates and his inexperience in Washington, far from being regarded as a handicap, was almost an asset to a disillusioned electorate, although Ford was personally unaffected by any 'Washington Miasma.'

Below: Nixon at the Great Wall of China in 1972. He was the first US president to visit China and was able to achieve a detente with that country. *Right:* Nixon was also the first American president to visit the Soviet Union. While there, he negotiated a partial strategic arms limitation agreement. *Opposite bottom:* Nixon aboard the *USS Hornet* greeting the returning astronauts following their lunar landing mission, 24 July 1969.

Left: Nixon announces his resignation, 9 August 1974. *Above:* Nixon and his wife, Pat, leaving the White House for the last time. They are accompanied by the Fords.

Top: Gerald R Ford on
9 August 1974 with Henry
Kissinger, the Secretary of
State. *Right:* Nixon
boarding his helicopter
after his resignation.

CARTER, A DEMOCRATIC INTERLUDE

Jimmy Carter was elected over Ford in America's bicentennial year. Like Lyndon Johnson he was free of the racial prejudices once common in the Deep South – in fact he was much concerned about civil rights not only in the United States but also in foreign lands.

But two specters haunted his administration. One was the economy. By a sort of paradox, the country, though generally prosperous as compared with most of the world, suffered from two hitherto opposite ills. In the past, boom times had meant not only full employment, high wages for the worker and high prices for the farmer, but also increased costs to the consumer. Depression years had meant unemployment, low prices and indebtedness. Now inflation continued, prices were high, but many were unemployed.

Right: The freed American hostages arriving from Iran at a US Air Base in West Germany, 22 January 1981.

Left: Jimmy and Rosalynn Carter. The Rev Jesse Jackson is in the rear to the right. *Above:* President Carter conducting a news conference on Iran.

The other difficulty came from Iran. The American government had given general support to Shah Reza Pahlevi, a vigorous and progressive, but harsh and ruthless, ruler. Revolution had made him an exile. The revolutionists desired to catch and punish the Shah, then in the United States. So a mob of fanatical Moslems seized the whole staff of the American embassy in Teheran and held them captive for 444 days as hostages for the return of the Shah. This was a gross violation of international law, but the president hesitated to act lest the mob kill the embassy staff before aid could reach far-away Iran. When at last Carter sent a rescue mission the expedition was unsuccessful.

In the meantime, the Shah had died in Egypt, but haggling over the conditions of release still continued. On the very day that Ronald Reagan, the newly elected President, took office, the hostages were at last set free. Some think that the Iranians chose the transition from one term to another with the double purpose of depriving Carter of any credit for getting the Americans free, and distracting attention from the celebration that is usual at the inauguration of a new president.

REAGAN, THE REPUBLICANS RETURN

In the election of 1980 Ronald Reagan was easily victorious over Carter; and the Republicans also gained the Senate and increased their minority contingent in the House of Representatives.

The new president, a former Hollywood actor and later governor of California, was a genial and friendly man, personally popular, and his popularity was enhanced by an attempt on his life. It did not seem to have

Left: Ronald Wilson Reagan, the fortieth president of the United States. *Above:* Reagan with his vice-president, George Bush. *Right:* Reagan making his first Inaugural Address, 20 January 1981.

been motivated by politics, since the would-be assassin claimed that he did it to attract the favor of an actress.

Early in his first term, Reagan was successful in getting a large part of his programs through a divided Congress. He severely cut all the federal social services, lowered certain tax rates and won senatorial approval for the sale of airplanes to Saudi Arabia. The assassination of the friendly Egyptian president, Anwar Sadat, had endangered America's position in the Middle East, and Reagan strove to build up new friendships among the Arab states without sacrificing America's commitments to maintaining the independence of the state of Israel.

His first term focused on the problems of checking Communism without war and stabilizing the economy.

Below: Ronald Reagan just before he was shot in the chest by a would-be assassin 30 March 1981. He is walking to his limousine following a speech at the Washington Hilton. *Right:* Reagan poses with the members of the United States Supreme Court. To the left of the president is Chief Justice Warren E Burger. Associate Justice

Thurgood Marshall (second from left) was the first black to serve on the court; Associate Justice Sandra Day O'Connor (to the right of the president) was the court's first woman, appointed by Reagan in 1981. *Below:* Police and secret service men converge on John W Hinckley just after he shot the president.

A TRANSITIONAL DECADE: THE 1980s

The late twentieth century has brought both progress and new problems to the American people. Foreign relations have been shadowed by continuing distrust between the United States and the Soviet Union, which has precluded the achievement of any meaningful agreement on nuclear arms control. US involvement in the troubled Middle East and Central America have entailed loss of American life and criticism in many quarters, both at home and abroad.

On the domestic scene, the influx of Spanish-speaking immigrants and refugees has made the Hispanic minority the fastest-growing in the nation. The greatest number of Spanish-speaking refugees were those from Castro's Cuba, which in 1983 showed signs of attempting to expand Soviet influence in the Western Hemisphere. The attempted takeover of the Caribbean island of Grenada by militant Marxist insurgents was attributed to the strong Cuban presence encountered there by US troops, who intervened to prevent establishment of a Communist Government and to rescue American medical students endangered by the revolution.

The 1980s brought heartening evidence that Americans were resolving domestic issues that had divided them in previous decades. The unveiling of the Vietnam Veterans Memorial in Washington, DC in 1982 symbolized some resolution of the deep bitterness engendered by the war. By that

Below: The Space Shuttle *Columbia* touching down in December 1983.

Above: A US-trained Salvadoran infantryman stands guard in his

troubled land.

Right: The ruins of the US Embassy in Beirut, Lebanon, after the 18 April 1983 bombing that killed over 50 people.

Left: Hispanic immigrants in a predominantly Cuban neighborhood near the Brooklyn Docks make a new place for themselves in America's largest city, home to generations of refugees.

Right: US 82nd Airborne troops use field communication gear to keep all units informed during the October 1983 invasion of Grenada, in which 1800 US and 300 Caribbean troops were involved.

Below: Many Vietnam veterans wept openly at the dedication of the stark and somber memorial to the 57,939 servicemen killed or missing in the divisive war in Southeast Asia. A total of 2.7 million Americans served in the conflict.

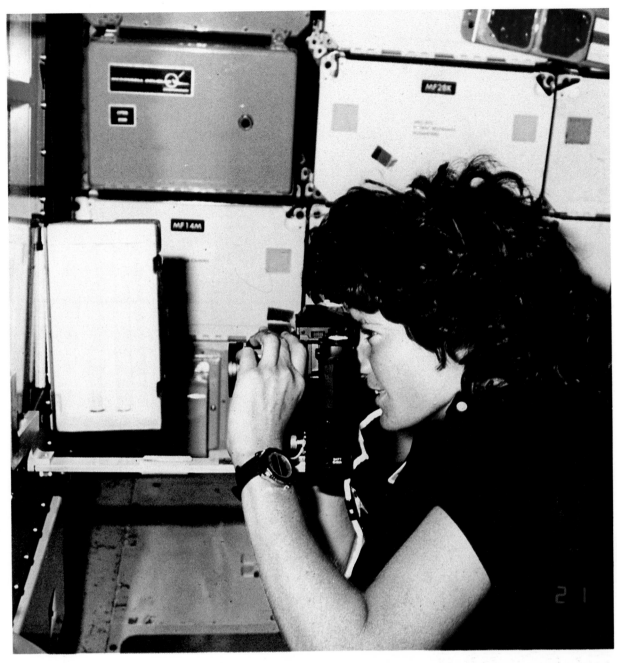

Above left: Former Vice-President Walter F Mondale and Representative Geraldine A Ferraro accept their party's nomination as candidates for the nation's highest offices in November 1984.

Above: The first woman in space, astronaut Sally K Ride, records the activity of a test specimen in her role as mission specialist aboard STS-7 in 1983.

Left: The 1984 Summer Olympics, held at Los Angeles, attracted participants from around the globe, despite the boycott by the USSR and 14 other communist nations.

Overleaf: The combination of Ronald Reagan and George Bush, Republican candidates for re-election in 1984, proved unbeatable.

time, most Vietnam veterans had re-entered the mainstream of American life, despite their own widespread ambivalence about the war and the mixed feelings they encountered when they first returned from it.

Ongoing progress in civil rights was manifested by the election of Harold Washington as the first black mayor of Chicago, a city historically characterized by strong and autonomous ethnic enclaves. Black leader Jesse Jackson was a candidate for the Democratic presidential nomination in the 1984 elections. The nomination was captured by former Vice-President Walter Mondale, who chose as his running mate the first major-party female candidate for vice-president, Representative Geraldine Ferraro of New York State. The Mondale-Ferraro ticket was overwhelmingly defeated by Republican candidates Ronald Reagan and George Bush, who returned to office with the largest electoral-college majority in American political history. A major factor in their re-election was economic recovery from the severe recession of the early 1980s, which was widely blamed on the previous administration.

A renewed spirit of patriotism manifested itself during the 1984 Olympic Games, held in Los Angeles in August and viewed by millions on national television. The Olympic Torch was carried across the country by an impressive array of American athletes, and the progress of its 'affirming flame' seemed to symbolize the national hope for a new era of American peace, prosperity and esteem within the community of nations.

LOOKING AHEAD

Since World War II the United States had become what Great Britain was in Queen Victoria's day – the center of the world's industry, commerce and finance. Although predominantly urban, it could still export wheat, fruit, farm produce and cotton, as well as manufactured goods.

Daring astronauts reached out into space. There had been a landing on the moon, and, even more remarkable, a successful return. Unmanned rockets went beyond Saturn. The newest device was a space shuttle that could soar into outer space and return accurately to a designated point.

But maturity brings responsibility. No one in 1776, and few in 1876, ever dreamed that the United States might become involved in wars in places as distant as Korea and Vietnam, or be threatened by war in Libya, Lebanon or Iran. As a leader in the United Nations, in the defensive North Atlantic Treaty Organization (NATO) and the Organization of American States (OAS), the United States had, in a sense, become the world's political, as well as economic, center.

In the early days of the republic, people who were discontented with their lot could always pull up stakes and move west. Now there was little land still open to settlement, save in distant Alaska. The United States' resources of mine, field and forest had seemed inexhaustible. Now the conservation of its rapidly dwindling natural resources had become urgent.

Fortunately, the nation's greatest resource – the spirit which always seeks new adventures and new challenges – still remains.

Below: For the first time, a photograph of four men who have served as president enjoying a moment of relaxation. *Right:* NASA's Voyager 2 took pictures of Saturn and its rings in August 1981.

INDEX

Page numbers in italics refer to captions to
illustrations